# Water off a Duck's Back

*How to deal with Frustrating Situations,*

*Awkward, Exasperating or*

*Manipulative People and...*

*Keep Smiling!*

## Jon Lavelle

First published in Great Britain on 21$^{st}$ June 2008

This revised edition published in Great Britain on
1$^{st}$ January 2010 by:

**Blue Ice Publishing Ltd.**

www.blueiceconsulting.co.uk

Reprinted 2011

Printed and bound in the UK by TJ International Ltd, Padstow, Cornwall

Registered UK Company
Registration No. 6436734
V.A.T. Registration: 925 8285 93

# Jon Lavelle

Author

Trainer

Facilitator

Key Note Speaker

Jon Lavelle is a rising authority in the fields of influence, negotiation, psychology, human relationships, persuasion, thinking and behaviour.

With an MBA from Warwick Business School, and eighteen years experience working in the field of Neuro-Linguisitic Programming (NLP), Jon elegantly combines rigorous theory with practical application. As a committed pragmatist, Jon's philosophy is... *"If it works... do it. If it doesn't... chuck it out and try something else – you have many more options than you might think!"*

Having facilitated groups and trained thousands of people across the world in business and life scenarios, Jon is well placed to know what works in practice, and what's a barmy old load of tosh!

Jon has worked in a number of leading global organisations specialising in management, leadership, communication skills and people-performance. He is an experienced facilitator and regular Key Note speaker at company functions and team-building events throughout Europe, the US and Asia.

Jon has previously published books in the areas of Learning & Development, Negotiation, Sales, Persuasion and Influence. The author can be contacted for enquiries relating to inspirational speaking engagements, or to discuss the concepts outlined in 'Water Off a Duck's Back', at... www.blueiceconsulting.co.uk

# Looking for a Key Note Speaker?

In-company Events, Industry Conferences, Team Days,
Product & Service Launches, Motivational Audience Events,
Inspirational Sales Conferences and more...

*"Jon's enthusiasm is infectious...
his workshops and facilitation
sessions sparkle with energy."*

Nick Fell
Chief Administration Officer, AET Group

*"Jon's commercial expertise, and
attention-grabbing, delivery style was
just what we needed for our Sales
and Key Account Team conferences."*

Matt Watkins
Sales Director, Teva Pharmaceuticals

*"Jon is personable and creative,
with a deep understanding of his
subject areas of influence,
persuasion, negotiation, psychology
and human behaviour."*

Nick Cole
Director – Direct Line Insurance

*"Jon really knows his
stuff, he's engaging,
thinks on his feet and
is hugely responsive to
his audience... be
prepared to be
challenged and
entertained!"*

Kath Rooney
Global Head of HR
International Shipping Group

*"Jon is such an energetic
speaker, with strong content
and logic to back it up, our
audiences are learning whilst
being inspired."*

James Zhang
Regional Director, Philips (China)

*"Energising, Engaging &
Enlightening - Hire him, you
won't be disappointed."*

Paul McGee - Author, speaker and
creator of SUMO (Shut Up Move On)

*To discuss your requirements for your next in-company or
conference speaking booking contact*

*www.blueiceconsulting.co.uk
jon@blueiceconsulting.co.uk*

# Thanks...

In no particular order... except the first mention... I would like to genuinely extend my heartfelt thanks to the following people, who have assisted in several ways in enabling me to nurture this 'baby' to maturity, both in print and in audio format:

**Julie** (my wife of 21 years) for being at my side, for trusting in my passion, in believing in my goals and ambition, even when the 'wolf was at the door' financially, and generally for being the 'Ying' to my 'Yang'! Thank you Julie, you give me the balance I need in decision-making, and in life in general. Together we make a great team... even though I do snore.

**Tanveer Choudhry** - Entrepreneur, for being an inspiration, a motivator, a friend, a harsh critic (for that, read 'friend'), and the provider of artwork, ideas and advice; you have been a great 'sounding board' for me Tanveer.

**Sarah Hellier** - for rising to the challenge of being the first to agree to 'appear' with me in the audio version of this book, and for being up for a curry with extra chillis!... though that's not quite so relevant; anyway, thank you Sarah.

**Andrew Bishop** - for standing in at the last moment to read some of the male voices in the audio book, and for rising to the occasion with such enthusiasm; thank you Andrew.

**Nancy Weibel** - for being Nancy. Those who know Nancy need no further introduction; but for those who don't, Nancy is an immensely caring and considerate friend; someone who I can rely on to help in a crisis... and... when there is no crisis; thank you Nancy.

**Paul Bromley** - Broadcaster and Journalist and, as I used to call him before I knew his real name... 'Mr. Sky Sports'. Paul gave unstintingly of his voice, lubricated it has to be admitted, with a rather rare Scottish Island Malt, to ensure that the audio version of this book slipped off the recording decks with resounding aplomb; you're a true professional, thank you Paul.

**Judi Hunter** - My sister, editor and proof reader, for reviewing the first draft and having a gentle hand on the tiller during the early versions of the book; thank you Judi for steering me in the right direction, and encouraging me to remove most of the swear words!

**Alison Eastwood** - Mrs 'Eagle Eyes' herself, who found errors in my manuscript that others missed. Nothing gets past you Alison, so thank you. Oh, and thank you for marrying my best mate, Dave... he was long over-due having someone sort him out!

**James Lavelle** - Band leader, guitarist and composer; and most importantly, owner of state of the art digital recording equipment which he let us borrow for the audio version! Thanks James.

Finally, I dedicate this book to all the frustrating, aggravating, irritating, devious and manipulative people out there who, for whatever reason, in their own small-minded, pitiful and misguided ways, either consciously or naively, make life more difficult than it needs to be.

I've got news guys; it might have worked for you in the past, but now we're wiser, smarter, better tooled up, and ready to take you on. From now on it's...

*...'Water off a Duck's Back!'*

# Water off a Duck's Back

*How to deal with Frustrating Situations,*

*Awkward, Exasperating or*

*Manipulative People and...*

*Keep Smiling!*

## Jon Lavelle

# Contents

# Chapter 1

Introduction

# 1 Introduction

## Victor's Vitriol

*"I don't believe it!"*

Victor Meldrew
'One Foot in the Grave' – BBC Television

No doubt, those of us familiar with the eternally frustrated, dumbfounded, irritated and aggrieved Victor Meldrew will have no trouble recollecting his famous catch phrase.

We've all been there haven't we; annoying, frustrating, aggravating or otherwise damned impossible situations. Circumstances where we simply cannot understand, why... *"For the love of God"*, (that's another of his favourites), we've got ourselves into a stressful pickle, or we're confronted with someone who's being particularly difficult.

Life happens; we drop our toast 'butter side down', as usual, or less politely a sticky, smelly substance hits the fan. For some people though, such as our eternally frustrated Victor, it seems to happen rather more often than mathematical chance would suggest is possible; some people just seem to attract trouble, don't they?

Do you know someone who always seems to find themselves in situations where they are compelled to complain? Nothing seems to go right for them, and whatever the circumstances you can pretty much be sure that they're going to be disappointed... often *massively*. How is it that other people don't seem to have quite so many things go so terribly wrong for them? With people such as this we might be tempted to ask... 'Hmmm, who's the common denominator in all of these situations?'

Assuming you're not a 'common denominator', but a regular person who suffers their fair share of life's frustrations and encounters with difficult people, you're probably keen to know how to deal with such situations without getting yourself worked up needlessly, stomping off in an indignant huff, saying something you later regret, or worse still, resorting to physical violence... again.

## It's Easy to Criticise a Chair

If you've visited a bookshop recently you will have noticed the plethora of 'rant books'. You know the sort of thing; books about gripes, indecencies, rudeness, poor grammar, misplaced ap'ost'rophy's', insulting behaviour, a decline in moral and social standards and general rudeness to one's fellow human being... or is it just the shelves that I'm drawn to?

Anyway, the books to which I refer are not 'self-help guides'; they don't tell you *how* to commit social indiscretions in restaurants, lifts, the office party or wherever. Nor do they give you top tips for how to embarrass customer service staff in public settings, or how to irritate readers with liberal smatterings of dangling participles or split infinitives. No, they are either lists of 'What's wrong with this country', barrages of vitriol which condemn bad manners, or self-righteous rants that aim to appeal to a higher code of conduct or sophisticated, increasingly rare morals.

What seems to be missing from this endless stream of 'complaint books' however, is any advice whatsoever on how to deal with all of this guff when it happens to you? How do you deflect life's 'slings and arrows', or avoid them being lobbed in your direction in the first place? How do you retain a degree of sanity, composure, control and self-assuredness in the midst of such fuss and frustration? How do you immunise yourself against idiots, shield yourself from charlatans and protect yourself from people who, for whatever reason, are trying to 'get at you'?

As my dad used to say… "It's easy to criticise a chair, but a damned site harder to make one." So, rather than a glossary of gripes and grumbles, think of this book as the solution to the broken chair. Not a rant about what's wrong with the world, but rather a self-help manual to fixing it (or at least your part in it), and fixing it for good.

As a general philosophy and approach to life, commit to being part of the solution, not a contributor to the problem.

So, in the spirit of trying to re-balance things, and to help those of us who want to learn how to deal more effectively with all the rubbish that's thrown at us, here's my collection of recipes for personal control, sanity, composure and peace of mind. A guide to rising above it all, actually *enjoying* the process of dealing with sticky situations and tricky tricksters, and emerging a stronger person as a result.

## Get Your Wand Out!

Get ready; you're about to perform 'magic', both on yourself, and on the people around you.

We're not talking about performing hypnotic stage magic like Darren Brown, or cunning stunts in the street. However, it will seem like magic once you try out some of the spells (tools and techniques) that we will discuss in the next few pages. We will also end the book with a particularly powerful spell from J.K.Rowling's now legendary Harry Potter; but for now...

We're going to discover a collection of state of the art psychological methods that are not only simple to apply, but also work in practice. You will learn to:

- Take greater control over how you think about what happens to you

- Explore a far wider range of options than you might have previously considered in terms of  how you respond to people and events

- Choose your specific response to people and situations, take control, exercise greater power

- Refuse to let anyone else control what you think and how you feel about things i.e. no-one can make you feel anything – unless you unwisely or unwittingly give them permission

- Learn to spot when people are playing 'mind games' with you, and know how to respond appropriately to diffuse the power of, or counter such gambits

- Build strong internal resistance and self-mastery; confident in your thinking, confident in yourself, and confident in your ability to deal effectively with what people and life throw at you - no matter how sticky!

- 'Think about your thinking' – explore new, empowering psychological strategies that will help you lead a happy and more successful life

- Learn state of the art methods of getting other people out of their small, limited, inaccurate, and often painful or negative perspectives on life's events and what's happening around them

- Spot the verbal mistakes that people make, or tricks they use, and counter these effectively, often with devastating and immediate effect; quite literally stopping people in their 'tracks'

- Deal with people who slander and slur others, exaggerate, make unfair judgements or connections, spread rumours or otherwise distort reality to their own ends
- Arm yourself with a comprehensive toolkit for pushing back assertively when you need to correct the inaccurate or unfair views of others; know how to 'set the record straight'
- Learn a set of proven techniques for dealing with unreasonable or objectionable people

If you don't give your brain a little direction then it will either run randomly on its own, or other people will find ways to run it for you, and they may not always have your best interests at heart.

From now on, you're going to experience life much more as a matter of choice.

You're going to be more in control of your reactions to people and events, you're going to feel a heightened sense of self-confidence and personal mastery, you're going to be more successful in your relationships and interactions with others, and above all else, you're going to be a happier person.

NB: Some of the more powerful techniques are described from Chapter 5 onwards. However, Chapters 2-4 are essential pre-reading to get you into the most resourceful state possible to make the very best use of your new 'magic tool kit'.

## Do You Enjoy Kipling?

Rudyard Kipling said it well when he wrote his famous poem, 'If'...

# If

*If you can keep your head when all about you*
*Are losing theirs and blaming it on you,*
*If you can trust yourself when all men doubt you,*
*But make allowance for their doubting too;*
*If you can wait and not be tired by waiting,*
*Or being lied about, don't deal in lies,*
*Or being hated, don't give way to hating,*
*And yet don't look too good, nor talk too wise:*

*If you can dream - and not make dreams your master,*
*If you can think - and not make thoughts your aim;*
*If you can meet with Triumph and Disaster*
*And treat those two impostors just the same;*
*If you can bear to hear the truth you've spoken*
*Twisted by knaves to make a trap for fools,*
*Or watch the things you gave your life to, broken,*
*And stoop and build 'em up with worn-out tools:*

*If you can make one heap of all your winnings*
*And risk it all on one turn of pitch-and-toss,*
*And lose, and start again at your beginnings*
*And never breath a word about your loss;*
*If you can force your heart and nerve and sinew*
*To serve your turn long after they are gone,*
*And so hold on when there is nothing in you*
*Except the Will which says to them: "Hold on!"*

*If you can talk with crowds and keep your virtue,*
*Or walk with kings - nor lose the common touch,*
*If neither foes nor loving friends can hurt you,*
*If all men count with you, but none too much;*
*If you can fill the unforgiving minute*
*With sixty seconds' worth of distance run,*
*Yours is the Earth and everything that's in it,*
*And - which is more - you'll be a Man, my son!*

Rudyard Kipling (1865-1936)

Inspired?

I hope so, as our journey of self-discovery and personal mastery is about to begin.

# Chapter 2

It's My Life

# 2 It's My Life

## Who's the Boss of You?

Let's start with a very fundamental, yet telling question: 'Who's in charge of your life?'

Now don't dismiss this in your hurry to read on; ask yourself honestly, 'How much of *me* do *I* control?'

For example, has anyone you know ever made you feel guilty, ashamed, irritated or angry? A no-brainer of a question I guess; so assuming the answer is "Yes" then join the club. If your answer is "Yes, every moment of my waking day, and often in my dreams", then it's possible that you might need more than just this book to help you.

Of course it's perfectly normal to feel such human emotions in response to other people's behaviour or their provocative comments. If someone insults you, for example, how else are you expected to feel, other than insulted?

However, my contention is that this 'perfectly normal' situation is most certainly not *'perfect'*, and neither is a *'normal'* reaction particularly helpful to you. To rise above such attacks requires a more elegant and sophisticated psychological and behavioural response. For example, it might be normal for millions of people to spend their evenings watching trashy, celebrity reality TV shows, or normal for kids to steal sweets from shops, but does that make it right? Does it mean that it's helping them in the long term?

So here's the first of many provocations that I will challenge you with throughout this book.

---

**Provocation** Reacting like a 'perfectly normal' human being can mean
 that you are conforming to, and reinforcing a dangerous
pattern of behaviour that does not help you, and even
worse, can actually harm you.

---

Here's the key... By reacting the way that most people do, you are conforming to what other people *want* you to do, and fully *expect* you to do. After all, why wouldn't they expect you to react that way? It's 'perfectly normal' to do so; they've learned this themselves from countless human interactions without you having to tell them.

However, if you react in a 'normal' manner, in the way that they expect, then you've already relinquished a degree of control. You're being led and influenced by someone else, and you may even be potentially falling into their trap - if they are cunning enough to lay such traps?

So, when the man holds the doggy treat high in the air, and the dog excitedly runs over, drools uncontrollably onto the kitchen floor and feels a rush of positive emotions... who's in control?

When your boss tells you that you should be ashamed of the quality of the piece of work that you've just submitted, and you sit there with your head low and eyes averted, shifting uneasily in your seat and feeling the weight of helplessness and inadequacy pressing down on your shoulders... who's in control?

When the boy-racer aggressor steams up behind you in the fast lane of the motorway, flashing his lights and driving on your tail; who's in control? By the way, we will be discussing a range of strategies for dealing with just such a situation in Chapter Six; but hang in here with me for now.

Yes, I know the answer to these questions is obvious, but here's the less-obvious, and sometimes hard part of this to grasp.

Aggressive acts and remarks, whether direct or indirect, are almost always used as a technique by the perpetrator to control a situation. They certainly have the potential power to do so, and they can easily put the recipient (you) on the back foot, un-nerved and forced to adopt a defensive position. Aggressive acts and remarks are pushy behaviours that attempt to dominate the other person, but, and this really, really, really is the hardest part of this to come to terms with and accept...

> **Provocation**    We almost always *choose* our emotional response to the
> ☞               situation in which we find ourselves.

Ok.... take a big breath.

If that's a provocation too far, just suspend your judgement for a moment. If it's too much to accept at face value, could you at least believe that it's possible for you to *learn* to choose your response, given some well-meaning advice and a bit of practice? Are you willing to be open-minded, if in doing so it will help you?

Are you open-minded about being open-minded?

Throughout this book, and particularly when we return to the subject in Chapter Nine, you will discover real life examples of how and where people have done this successfully. It might help you to think of it like this...

If you feel 'guilty' about something then it is you who is making yourself feel guilty. Nobody can do anything to *make* you feel guilty, or to force you to experience any other emotion for that matter, unless you *allow* yourself to feel guilty.

Can you make someone love you? Of course not. I once tried desperately to get someone to love me, by constantly being around them, buying presents and huge cards with love hearts and teddy bears on. I used to leave love notes in their handbag at work, flowers under their windscreen wipers in the car park, and post chocolates through their letter-box. I began following them around out of work so that I could feign a chance encounter in a coffee shop or in the public library. After all, who wouldn't love that amount of attention? She moved away without leaving a forwarding address. What strange behaviour?

Anyway, back to feeling 'guilty', can you make someone feel guilty?

Just examine the words... 'feel guilty'. It is you who owns your feelings so it is you who is doing the feeling!

To put it another way, you may have done something that you shouldn't, or you may have let someone down, but 'guilt' is only one of a range of emotions and reactions that you could choose to adopt. How about choosing to respond with feelings of regret, confusion, arrogance, disbelief, curiosity, ambivalence, or just plain 'sorry'? If you're in charge of your own emotions and reactions then you should have a degree of choice, surely?

This morning my wife, Julie, woke up and said that she felt guilty for letting down her co-helpers at the church coffee morning (she had the flu and could not muster the energy to go in). My response was to ask her to replace any feelings of guilt with a feeling of liberation, as for once in her life she could lie in bed while someone else does all the organising of the tea and coffee. Our conversation passed on to other matters, and it was some fifteen minutes later that I asked her how she was now feeling? "Liberated" she exclaimed, with a big smile on her face. We both laughed at her response, which in a sense just goes to show how we can beat ourselves up with feelings that are not only undeserved, they are also unhelpful... to all concerned.

Now here's the first of many 'Health Warnings' that I will be tempering some of my advice and techniques with.

 **Health Warning**

Some politicians are so thick skinned that they have difficulty in even *pretending* to be sorry when they are not! The best that you will get from the majority of politicians is regret that their action has created a response or reaction in others. You will hardly ever hear them regret an action that they have taken, and admit to being genuinely sorry about what they did. Their regret is for how others have reacted to what they have done, or regret for 'regrettable circumstances', rather than any specific and personal apology for their own behaviour.

"I regret the way in which the honourable lady has responded to these events" is not the same as saying "I am sorry for doing XYZ and I apologise to the honourable lady for any upset I may have caused."

Of course, the 2009 MP's expenses scandal in the UK exposed many MPs for what they are, and provided numerous opportunities for MPs to say "Sorry". Unfortunately, the closest that most came to this was an admission that ... "There appears to have been an administrative error", references to an "Oversight" or an "Error of judgement".

In stark contrast, we occasionally see senior members of Japanese industry or government falling on their sword – sometimes quite literally. There are several instances of Japanese business leaders breaking down emotionally in front of cameras, because they cannot handle the sheer guilt and humiliation of letting down employees. In November 2009 a Japanese politician was found hanged after admitting widespread fraud.

Now politicians are a breed to themselves a fascinating group to study. They are masters of, or have at least been trained in the tricks and techniques of manipulation, spin and evasion. As soon as you try to pin them down it feels like you're grappling with a snake in a tub of warm Vaseline. NB, if you've never tried this, to avoid unnecessary mess, cover your carpets and furniture with dust sheets first.

So, my 'Health Warning' is not to take things to extremes. Don't become too cool, calculating, cold, disengaged from your emotions, or inhuman in your reactions and responses to people and events. If you do, then you will probably lead an increasingly lonely life.

What I want you to do is to think about how you react to the actions and comments of others, and to ask yourself simply whether your typical, instinctual reactions either help you, or hinder you?

If you feel intimidated it is because you are allowing yourself to feel intimidated – period! Another person in the same situation, or even yourself on a totally different occasion, might stand their ground, argue back, shrug their shoulders, go for a beer, admit that "There seems to have been a communication breakdown here", sit down and have a sensible discussion, or try to negotiate a mutually acceptable solution.

If you feel angry it is because you have chosen to become angry. You have chosen to react to the behaviour or comments of another person, or the situation that you find yourself in, by thinking the thoughts that you do, feelings the emotions you choose, or by doing the things you decide to do.

If, like most people, you are already reacting to this by saying things like "Of course he makes me angry, who wouldn't get angry considering what he did! How the hell was I expected to feel? *Overjoyed!?", t*hen remember that this response is also 'perfectly normal'; that's why I'm anticipating that some may find this concept psychologically challenging, at least initially.

So it's a perfectly normal reaction. Err…, we've been here before, haven't we?

If you're still not convinced then that's probably because you're now thinking of extreme scenarios, such as someone pulling a gun on you in a dark alley, being sacked from your job, learning that someone close to you is dying of a terminal illness or that your neighbour is a child abductor. But remember, my proposition is that we can *almost always* choose our emotional response. There are going to be extreme examples which disprove the general rule, but we're talking here about surviving day-to-day trials and tribulations, not of dealing with psychotically disturbed individuals who deserve every punishment that society can meter out to them. That said, in Chapter Nine we will take a look at some stronger tactics that you can use on the (hopefully) few occasions that you encounter where more potent actions are required.

In the world of 'psychological sword fighting' there are few hard and fast rules, and sometimes breaking a rule that has been assumed, for example by doing what the other person least expects, can have effective and dramatic results.

So remember, the currency I'm dealing in here is the currency of provocation and challenging ideas. Not everything will work with every person in every situation, and in a sense the only rule is that there are no rules. In fact to be too 'rule-bound' is to be needlessly self-bound and self-restricted in the responses available to you.

In the most challenging situations it's a dangerous game of attack, parry, defence and counter attack, and the winner will be the person who can keep their cool and employ the widest range of techniques and strategies against psychologically wilful opponents.

## "Tell Me How to Feel ... *Please*"

If you're still in doubt about your ability to choose your response then you're essentially admitting that you're allowing other people to control how you feel about things; which is a little bit feeble, isn't it?

I began this book with a light-hearted reference to a well loved comic character, Victor Meldrew. I now want to take a more serious tack by drawing your attention to another Victor, with a slightly different spelling.

Viktor Frankl, a famous Jewish survivor of the Nazi death camps, is probably one of the best known testaments to the power of choosing your reactions to what life throws at you. If you're interested you should read his books which recount in some detail his experiences of retaining self-control in extreme circumstances. The key message however is his 'Stimulus-Response' theory in which he asserts that between any external stimulus and the subsequent human response lies the concept of human choice.

In most circumstances we have a choice as to how we respond to a stimulus. Remember my earlier Health Warning; I said in '*most*' circumstances.

The dog that salivates in response to the expectation of food has a more primitive Pavlovian response, but in humans we have the ability to moderate our primeval responses with intelligent thought; well most of us do anyway.

So, yet again we learn that nobody can *make* us feel things; we *decide* how we feel in response to other people's behaviour. To argue otherwise is to admit that we are pre-programmed automatons acting against our will, or that our emotions and feelings can be triggered by other people as easily as if they'd flicked a switch in our minds. We know this already as it's ingrained in our language in phrases such as:

- "Who's pushed your buttons then?"
- "Someone's touched a raw nerve with you, haven't they?"
- "How come you're being so touchy?"

Just reading the three expressions above may have had an effect upon you.

Some people report a prickly feeling in the hairs on the back of their neck when reading or hearing such expressions directed at them. Maybe you feel the same when thinking about such scenarios, or you find yourself sliding into a defensive or irritated state. Remember, you're only reading a book, you're not the person being accused of being out of control, childish or whatever slur is inferred by such remarks. However, somehow those words have the ability to raise our hackles, even when written in sterile print.

It's not what happens to you, but rather how you react to what happens to you that's important. It's not what people say or do to you, but how you choose to react to those behaviours that's important, and that's what determines the outcome.

Frankl's most significant insight from his years of incarceration was that no matter what anyone did, they could not take away what he called his one, ultimate personal freedom – his ability to *choose his response* to the situation in which he found himself.

> "*The one thing you can't take away from me is the way I choose to respond to what you do to me. The last of one's freedoms is to choose one's attitude in any given circumstance.*"

Viktor Frankl
Austrian psychiatrist and psychotherapist: 1905-1997

| | |
|---|---|
| **Tactic:**  | Recognise that between 'stimulus' and 'response' is a gap, an opportunity for you to pause and to consider how you will respond. |
| | Practise using the gap to think, before you respond, and lengthen the amount of time you have by getting into the habit of pausing. The extra thinking time, even if only momentary, means you're likely to make a more intelligent and helpful response. |

Like Frankl, I want to take us to a deeper level; away from the normal surface reactions we have in response to daily irritations and annoyances, and to examine more closely just how 'in control' we truly are capable of becoming. I want to show you, through practical examples and simple techniques, how quickly and easily you can take charge of your thoughts, feelings, emotions, reactions and behaviour.

As you've seen earlier, and will throughout the remainder of this book, I have tried to bring the tactics, techniques and ideas to life by relating them to personal examples and incidents within my own experience. In this way I hope, not only to give these ideas vibrancy and meaning, but also to demonstrate to you, the reader, that I practise what I preach... most of the time!

I don't know whether you will be more amazed by the power of the techniques we are going to discover, or by the speed with which they will work for you? What I do know, is that by applying just some of what you are beginning to learn here you will emerge a more confident, assertive, controlled, and dare I say 'happier' person as a result.

Sounds like a worthwhile exploration doesn't it?

Unlike thousands of his less fortunate fellow prisoners, Frankl's story is an inspiration to us all. After all, it's the ultimate confirmation that his assertion works, as unlike tens of thousands of his fellow prisoners, he survived to tell the tale.

What better proof can there be?

| | |
|---|---|
| **Provocation** <br>  | Nobody can make you feel things; you decide how you feel in response to life events and other people's behaviour. |

If you don't give your brain a little direction then it will either run randomly on its own, or other people will find ways to run it for you, and they may not always have your best interests at heart.

Decide to experience life much more as a matter of choice, rather than just letting things happen to you, or simply blowing with the wind.

In Chapter 3 we are going to explore how we can start to take more control over what happens to us, our reactions to people and events, and begin to broaden our repertoire of responses that help, not hinder us.

# Chapter 3

## Sticks & Stones

# 3
# Sticks & Stones

## Nursery Crimes

*"Sticks and stones may break my bones, but words can never hurt me"*
Playground chant

We all know the schoolyard chant, but how many of us take heed of, and truly internalise this philosophy? It can be hard, very hard indeed to dismiss personal slurs or insults because they are just that; personal and potentially insulting.

Children can be cruel; we only have to observe kids in the playground to see just how cruel, yet adults, who should know better, can engage in verbal attacks that are just as cutting.

On a scale of 1 (un-concerned) to 10 (livid), how do you feel when someone insults your:

- Continent
- Country
- Prime Minister or a member of your favoured political party
- National culture
- National cuisine
- Company you work for

- Acquaintances

- Mother-in-law

- Friends

- Choice of television viewing

- Sunglasses

- Neighbourhood

- Dress sense

- Habits

- Haircut

- Physique

- Personal hygiene

- Intelligence

- Mother

- Wife, Husband or Partner

- Children

My guess is that there are insults that you laugh at or even agree with, and there are others that impel you to lurch at the other person with rage. Perhaps you became more defensive as you read down the list as the subject matter became progressively more personal in nature or 'closer to home'.

Some insults are just too much to take, particularly when they get personal. They trigger within us a Neanderthal-like reflexive response which causes us to react impulsively, often without thinking. In a sense we are momentarily thrown out of our personal 'driving seat' as our primordial emotions take over. We will return to the subject of insults in Chapter Nine.

A colleague in Asia, who I may only see a couple of times a year, recently greeted me with... "Hi Jon; hey you've put on a bit of weight since I last saw you. Have you filled out a bit?"

He wasn't joking.

Even though he was right (I had put on a couple of kilograms since I was last in Asia), this did not stop me from reacting defensively. I told him that it wasn't a very nice thing to say, even if it was true, and suffice to say, our meeting didn't exactly get off to a good start. However, what was even more concerning was the number of times I thought about the incident during the rest of the week. It really threw me off my stride and made me question whether I was letting myself go in other ways?

At that time I could have done with taking the advice of Christina Aguilera, in her song 'Beautiful'...

> *"You are beautiful, no matter what they say*
> *'Cause words can't bring you down.*
> *We are beautiful, in every single way;*
> *'Cause words can't bring us down."*
>
> Christina Aguilera

---

**Tactic:**       Take some advice from Christina Aguilera's 'Beautiful' track.

She also did quite a funky number called 'Dirty'
- but that's not quite so relevant!

---

## Fight or Flight?

You may be familiar with the deep seated 'fight or flight' response that has been programmed into us, not only from birth, but as part of our evolution as a human species. Without such an immediate and powerful response to real or perceived danger then we would not have survived as a species; our ancestors would quite literally been someone else's breakfast!

The difference is that in the modern world we are rarely immediately confronted with violent or physical attacks that require an equally strong physical reaction. What we face in today's society are attacks of a different nature, be they verbal comments, inconsiderate behaviour, petty rudeness, awkward people and those who seek to manipulate us to their own ends.

Since prehistoric times, our minds and bodies have not evolved as fast as the changing environmental threats that we face in the modern world. Tyrannosaurus Rex may not be around to chew on us for breakfast, but we can be left with a feeling that we've been mauled alive by the boss!

So, recognising that much of our natural, human reaction to events is pre-programmed into us, and hence 'natural', this section comes with another 'Health Warning':

| | |
|---|---|
| **Remember:**  | As an emotional human being it is impossible for you to be totally devoid of feelings and natural emotions; you are not a 'robot' and neither should you try to behave like one. |

So, within this context, the challenge is in being able to contain and control our natural (for this read 'potentially damaging') human instinctual and emotional reactions, thus being able to retain a degree of composure in the face of provocation. You almost have to metaphorically 'lift yourself out of yourself'.

*"Listen love, in the cut and thrust of a live chat show,*
*people are going to get hit;*
*If you can't stand the heat, get out of the kitchen."*

Alan Partridge
'Knowing Me Knowing You' – BBC Radio 4

Punching someone in the face is extremely unlikely to result in a happy outcome for anyone concerned. Equally, however, allowing yourself to become privately irritated by someone else's behaviour can only damage you from the inside-out, eat away at you insidiously and almost certainly result in you feeling bad. The key question to address here is...

*"Why would anyone want to make themselves feel bad?"*

## People Play 'Mind Games'

Do you mind games?                          Are you game?

Do you mind playing?                        Do you engage in 'mind playing'?

Are you game for a match?                   Are you a match for the game?

What's your game?                           Are you fair game?

Are your games fair?                        Game, set and match!

Wouldn't life be so much easier if people didn't play mind games? I guess, but then it may also be a little boring.

In the real world an absence of mind games is an unrealistic expectation, as is a universal belief that everyone can be trusted, and we often find ourselves getting caught up in psychological games, even when we're not the initiators.

As with an alcoholic, 'awareness is half of the solution'; and this is particularly the case in learning to deal with the mind games of others. If you are aware that mind games are being played upon you, and you know what the other person is trying to achieve by doing this, then much of their power simply evaporates.

People who maliciously play mind games are trying to manipulate others; but before we write off these psychological jousts as completely underhand and without value, it's worth considering the many ways in which they can be useful.

For example, consider what goes on during the initial stages of a dating process? The idea that someone is, or is not interested in you will have an impact upon how much you like them, and upon how you then respond to them; unless of course, you were the girl that I had my heart set on all those years ago, when my excessive attention and obsessive compulsion led to repulsion rather than romance.

If someone plays 'hard to get' (a conscious mind game in which an individual acts out behaviours that are either neutral, or the opposite of how they are actually feeling) then this can potentially increase your affection for them and your determination to succeed in winning them over. This is a perfect example of a 'mind game' because one person is pretending to feel the opposite of how they actually feel. Now if that's not manipulation and distortion then I don't know what is, yet it's a remarkably common, apparently counter-intuitive behaviour.
Why should someone behave in this way?

Because counter-intuitive or not, where humans are involved it often works! We're both complex and simple at the same time.

If you're interested in the underlying psychology, it's related to the principle of 'scarcity', whereby the more unattainable something is perceived to be, the more its value increases in the eye of the beholder. If it's the 'last one in the shop' then you will fight harder to ensure that you get hold of it, ahead of anyone else, and rationality and logic tend to fly out of the window. Put simply, if something is exclusive then it increases in perceived value simply because of its exclusivity, even though nothing material has changed.

Artwork is a classic example. When two rich bidders set their heart on a unique piece by Damien Hurst in 2008, the price rocketed way beyond initial art expert estimates of its value.

Witness the countless examples of desperate parents who get close to Christmas and who are willing to pay well over the odds for hard to get items for their children. This happened with physical toys such as Pokemon characters or Transformers years ago, and can now be witnessed as people clamour over the latest computer games console, virtual reality game or i-Phone.

Switching from software games to human psychological games, we know that any game or manipulative ploy can backfire... therein lies the danger and intrigue of playing a game. In the case of the person on the receiving end of the 'hard to get' mind game, they may simply decide that the other person really isn't interested in them, they may consider that it's just too much trouble to pursue them, or at a higher level, they recognise the game for what it is and simply refuse to 'play'. In this case the second person is playing a mind game of their own; let's call it a 'two can play at that game' strategy, a game of bluff and counter-bluff; a game within a game. Unfortunately, in this case, the mutual games become counter-productive and neither person wins.

So we see how easy it is to be drawn into playing a mind game that is not of our own making, of how we can be carried along with the game-playing, of how we can stage our own counter-games in response, and of how it can all backfire and we wonder what on Earth we were 'playing at'? Importantly, in the heat of the situation this doesn't always happen at a conscious level, or at least at a level at which we can truly profess to be in full control of our thinking and our actions.

There is not necessarily any malice intended in the sort of mind game described above. There's no overt intention to hurt or disadvantage another person; it's more a case of 'psychological dancing', of covert influence, or good natured well-intentioned tomfoolery. Think of it as the modern day equivalent of the masked ball of Shakespearian times, in which potential suitors hid behind masks, not wishing to reveal their true identities and feelings; at least not initially. However, as is also sometimes portrayed by Shakespeare, by hiding behind a mask the wrong person gets a knife in the heart.

Another familiar example is the mind game that's played between people exchanging presents. Here, the rules of the mind game are to exaggerate the perceived value of the gift you receive, even, and this is the farcical part of this game, if you don't want, need or like the item.

Come on, admit it. We've all played along with this game in the past, because not to do so would have serious negative consequences for some of our most important relationships.

The second part of this mind game is to play down the value of the gift that you have given to the other person as in... "Oh, it's nothing special, I hope you like it, but I wasn't entirely sure, you can always take it back if you want – I've kept the receipt."

Here the unspoken deal is "Help me to save face and I'll help you to do the same; let's both fool each other without admitting it to anyone, including ourselves." We'll both carry on in blissful ignorance whilst paradoxically we're both fully aware of what's going on; a strange, but at the same time entirely familiar state of affairs – a 'game'.

And one more example; imagine two female friends meeting in the street...

Emily:     *"Hi Sylvia. My you look good; have you lost a few pounds recently?"*

Sylvia:    *"Goodness, no. I don't think so, I still struggle to get into this dress; but you're looking great, the diet's obviously working since I last saw you."*

Emily:     *"No, you really do look good. I'm afraid chocolate still holds sway in my life, I'm going to have to go on the 'Cabbage Soup Diet' again!"*

This is what is outwardly expressed. What is inwardly thought is more like:

Emily:     *'Good God, Sylvia's let herself go a bit.'*

Sylvia:    *'If I play down her compliment then it will make Emily insist even more strongly how slim I look, and if I compliment her then she will dismiss it, and say that she's still struggling to lose weight.'*

Emily:     *'I'll tell her again how good she looks, so that she doesn't make any effort to lose weight and continues to look overweight in comparison to me.'*

Okay, I might be exaggerating, but it shows that on the surface at least, some mind games can be useful in preserving relationships, or in avoiding ungainly fist fights or hair-pulling in the street. Many are nothing more than a natural part of how we have learned to interact and get along in society. After all, what's the alternative?

| | |
|---|---|
| Emily: | *"Hi Sylvia... have you put on weight since I last saw you?"* |
| Sylvia: | *"Well, maybe a few pounds, but you're hardly catwalk material."* |
| Emily: | *"No, but at least I don't look like I've put my makeup on in the dark."* |
| Sylvia: | *"You bitch, my husband always said you were a tart."* |
| Emily: | *"Yes, and he'd know about that wouldn't he, especially after we spend the night together at the Hemel Hempstead Travel Lodge last week."* |
| Sylvia: | [Shocked silence] |
| | *"Right, well at least that explains where he caught the clap."* |

I was at a dinner some time ago, hosted by one of my suppliers. They had provided drinks and a nice meal in a posh London hotel, and paid for an eminent guest speaker. Whilst the food, drink and company were great, unfortunately the evening was let down by the poor quality of the speaker, in terms of both delivery and content. His job title was 'Professor of Innovation' for a leading Business School, but unfortunately, he had little to say that could be categorised as innovative.

Next to me was a lady who was sat next to the Managing Director of the company who was hosting the event. She was saying how much she was enjoying the evening and how interesting the speaker had been. As I disagreed, and in fact could not identify a single thing that I had learned from the speech I challenged her on her assertion that she had found it interesting, and what it was that she had learned from the speech that she found to be useful? She was completely unable to answer the question; much to her embarrassment, the MD of the company... and myself!

Lesson to self:     Sometimes it's best just to tell people what they want to
                    hear i.e. games are a dish best served warm rather than
                    cold.

So, as this specific example shows, many people will lie in order to be polite in
polite company, and not to cause a fuss. Unfortunately, there are unintended
consequences, as if her assertion had gone unchallenged then the MD would
have re-booked the speaker for the following year's dinner, and proceeded to
bore most of his customers for a second year running... if they had bothered
to turn up or even remain his customers.

The positive side of this true life incident however, is that it spurred the MD to
work the room after the speech and seek genuine feedback from the
participants on the basis of... "I don't want you to be polite, I genuinely want
you to be honest in your feedback." Needless to say, by the end of the
evening he had decided that the speaker had not gone down well with his
audience, something that he might not have realised if he had simply taken
my dinner partner's comments at face value.

In trying to be 'nice' it's also possible to be inadvertently cruel by, in this
instance, not giving someone the thing that they really need.

Putting polite niceties and social lubrication aside for a moment, what about
more troublesome or unhelpful mind games? What about the malicious mind
games associated with bullying, backstabbing, belittling, blackmailing,
gossiping, laying guilt trips, blaming others and general bad mouthing? These
are all examples of ways in which people use mind games to damage the
reputation of, or intentionally hurt other people.

It is these less than helpful, or downright destructive mind games to which we
now turn our attention.

## Awareness is Half the Solution

Assuming we realise that a person is using a mind game upon us i.e. we are aware of what is happening, just as the alcoholic becomes aware that they really do have a problem, then this gives us a psychological advantage which enables us to move to the next stage of tackling mind games. This involves uncovering and understanding what the person is hoping to achieve by behaving in such a manner.

Firstly, let's understand that when a person bullies someone they are doing it to exert control over them, to have their own way or to demonstrate power. When someone back-stabs, gossips about, badmouths or belittles another person, they are doing it in order to appear better than them; relatively speaking they're trying to raise themselves up by putting someone else down. They try to elevate themselves by metaphorically stepping on other people's heads.

A truly decent person on the other hand, gain respect by helping others to climb higher *with them*.

When someone blames or guilt trips another person they're doing it from a position of moral inferiority, and by using negative 'attack weapons' to try to gain control over their victim's feelings; they want the person to be emotionally hurt in some way.

By taking the above examples we can see that destructive mind games are about one individual dominating another, making themselves appear better than that person in some way(s), or about exerting control and power over another's emotions.

So if that's what they are trying to achieve, what could be the root cause of this behaviour?

What all of these behaviours ultimately derive from is a sense of insecurity on the part of the perpetrator. People who play mind games, do so because it helps them to hide their own insecurity. They feel that by demonstrating the opposite traits they won't be found out for who or what they really are.

---

**Remember:** People who use mind games often do so because it hides
 their own sense of insecurity and inferiority

---

In William Shakespeare's Hamlet we find the line:

*"The lady doth protest too much."*

In other words, the more a person tries to portray themselves or a situation in one way, the more it becomes obvious that the opposite could in fact be true. The more one protests to be one thing, the more it becomes obvious that they are not. For example, the more a defendant protests their innocence, the more some people will tend to think they are guilty.

In the marketing and commercial world there's a concept of 'shouting too much' which can become self-defeating. If you try too hard to tell your customers what you are then you risk raising suspicions in the minds of your customers that the reason you're trying to hard is because you're over-compensating for what you're not! In marketing, subtle is often best.

In day to day speech you will often hear people saying things like "I'm not being difficult, but…", or "I don't mean to complain, but…" When you hear expressions such as these you know that immediately following the word 'but' will be some form of disqualifier, excuse or complaint. They then immediately go on to demonstrate the exact attitude or behaviour that they are openly saying they do not possess. It's similar to the dating mind game we explored above, only in this case the deception is more clumsy, more transparent, and easier to expose. This is because a person cannot say "I'm not being difficult" without using the word 'difficult', and in so doing they put the concept of difficulty out in the open! A person cannot say "I don't mean to complain, but..." without turning the subject to one of complaining.

I was in a meeting recently when someone said "If I was an Accountant... and I really don't mean to be rude... but...", and they were immediately interrupted by an Accountant who said... "Well, after that opening phrase almost anything that you say subsequently is likely to be insulting!" On this occasion it was a good-humoured interchange, but it illustrates the point.

Here are a couple more everyday examples that illustrate this psychological phenomenon.

How often, when you see a sign that says 'Wet Paint – Please Don't Touch' do you feel compelled to touch, if only just a tiny bit, in order to check if it's still wet? Even if it was wet, in what way does this confirmation of something that you already know help you? It's similar psychology at work. The human mind cannot think in negatives so, for example, if you were asked not to think about your front door, you would have to think about your front door in order to understand the command not to think about it, but by then it's too late! An acquaintance of mine was complaining some time ago about feeling 'trapped at work'. They worked for a large multi-national company, and had done so for 18 years. They were deeply unhappy, and had wanted to quit for a few years, but had not done so. Whenever the subject came up in conversation she reinforced the fact that she was not hanging on in the hope of a pay-off (voluntary redundancy), and that it wasn't a 'money thing'.

On one occasion it really did seem to be a case of 'The lady doth protest too much' and so I called her on it, saying that I did not believe her, and the fact that she mentioned it every time we spoke about her situation led me to believe that it was exactly the hope of a pay-off that was keeping her in her unhappy predicament. "Come on Sharon, admit it. The only reason you're still with XYY Ltd. is because you want to be paid off, and to resign voluntarily would mean that you're walking away from that possibility in the future, and, the more you go on denying this to yourself, the more entrapped you will become. Am I right?"

After a pause she admitted that I was right. Not only was she trying to deny this to her friends, she was also fooling herself.

Sad as this situation is, Sharon was not playing a malicious mind game. However, she was playing a mind game of sorts, a game in which she fools herself... what's that all about!?

Back in the sphere of manipulative mind games, as long as you remain conscious and aware of these signs, use them to alert you to the fact that a person is playing a mind game, and remember that this is not a sign of strength, but rather they're telegraphing insecurity, then you will be able to keep a cool head. Mind games can only work against you if you let them, and so the first option open to you is simply refuse to play.

| | |
|---|---|
| **Tactic:**  | When confronted with a malicious or unhelpful mind game, just refuse to play. By refusing to play, the game falls apart. |

It's often said that 'it takes two to tango'. Just as it takes two people to create a fight or an argument, or two people to play tennis, it takes at least two people to play a mind game. The exception, as illustrated above, is when a person is fooling themselves, subject that we will return to later.

Generally speaking though, playing solo just isn't fun in the world of human relationships! If one person refuses to play then the game falls apart, or at least that particular game falls apart, leaving the game initiator up a blind alley with fewer options. We will return to this tactic in Chapter Nine when we discuss more elaborate ways of 'not playing'.

When you realise the insignificance of the petty, psychological one-upmanship of others, and how childish it can be to play such games, you can start to lift yourself above such tomfoolery and to focus upon what's really important to you in any situation or any given relationship.

At the end of the day who really cares if another person *thinks* that they are getting one up on you? Far more important questions are *have* they got one up on you, and if so, does it *really* matter in the grand scheme of things?

That said, I'm not suggesting that you simply walk away from mind games without dealing with any problems that they may create, and I am certainly not advocating the childish, emotionally unintelligent response of 'taking your toys home' or 'throwing your dummy out of the pram'. What you need to do is to reach the point where you can ignore the mind game, whilst at the same time, deal in your own controlled way with any problems that accompany it.

For example, if you are being badmouthed it's important to defend yourself, but in doing so it's essential that you don't get yourself caught up in the politics. Simply let yourself be aware of the impact the badmouthing comments might have, and then coolly and calmly lay out the facts as accurately as you can. Separate facts from claims, the truth from bitching and make this clear to whoever is relevant and needs to hear it.

| Tactic:  | Refuse to play the mind game, and instead focus your energy and response on redressing any misrepresentation of yourself by laying out the facts and presenting these to the people who matter. |
|---|---|

Far too often we let ourselves get caught up in what everyone else thinks and in how 'important' we think we are. This is a double-whammy of a time waster, and another example of how it's possible to play mind games with ourselves.

We shouldn't need validation from other people to know that we are good, worthy or intelligent. What's essential to realise is that we are good when we do good things, and we know when we do good things. We are worthy when we do worthy things, and we recognise these. We are intelligent when we do intelligent things, and we know when we're acting intelligently.

Once you get to the stage where you're aware of such things, you can concentrate on feeling good yourself and letting people get on and do what they do without letting them affect you. At this stage you have true control, and no matter what other people's illusions of control and power they may have over you, you can simply roll with it, stay focused on doing all you can do, and be all you can be for yourself and for those who are important in your life.

It's also very important to ensure that you maintain a polite respect for such people. Any demonstration of anger, irritation or abusive behaviour on your side demonstrates that you're losing some control and they're 'winning', which potentially gives them further ammunition. When you can smile and go about your business in a relaxed way then it is you who will win in the long run; remember Rudyard Kipling.

Returning to our 'nursery crimes' and the 'sticks and stones' philosophy, there's a message there for us all, and more than a hint at a solution. However, as human beings that live and work with others in the 'real world', not the imaginary one of fairy tales and nursery rhymes, we must recognise that there will be occasions when the spiteful and hurtful words of others will cut deep; not physically of course, though words can be as cutting as the most piercing rapier. We only have to examine everyday language to clearly see this. Expressions such as "I was cut to the quick", "She was having a dig at me", "He cut me down with a single word", "It was daggers out" and "She really stuck the knife in" are commonly heard. Yesterday a colleague told me that he had just had his "Balls cut off"!

Really?

In Chapter Seven we will look at how to deal with cutting language, but for now, accepting that words do have the *potential* to strike deeply, and building upon Victor Frankl's philosophy, my provocation here is:

| **Provocation** ☞ | Nobody can hurt you with words, unless you *allow* them to. |
|---|---|

The key message here is the second part of the sentence, 'unless you *allow* them to.'

Okay, it's simple to say, not necessarily easy in practice, so what else can we do at a practical level to build up our immunity to such cutting remarks?

In the next chapter I will use the world of computers to draw some analogies and to provide some more practical tips, tactics and solutions.

# Chapter 4

## Building Inner Resilience & Power

# 4
# Building Inner Resilience & Power

## 'System Administrator' Rights

In any computer network the 'System Administrator' is the Supreme Being, they have 'Access All Areas' and can do pretty much whatever they want - unchecked. So the first step is to (re)claim your birth-given right as System Administrator for your own mind and body.

> **Provocation**
>       You are your own 'System Administrator'

Earlier we discussed the fact that you are (or should be) the boss of your own life, so now lets reinforce this theme with some practical tools that you can use to protect yourself from unwelcome attacks – just as you would protect your computer from a virus, Trojan Horses and the like.

So, firstly accept that, barring unfortunate accidents and uncontrollable diseases, you are the Master Programmer of your life and your future. If, at this early stage you cannot accept this then you need to do some serious rethinking, and you're unlikely to find all the answers that you need within the covers of this book.

Assuming you're still with me, let's delve a little deeper.

Even vast corporate networks become infected and corrupted by viruses; the most encrypted digital fortress can become a victim of a determined and unscrupulous hacker. You too are at risk, maybe more so, as a fleshy vulnerable human being.

However, just like a computer you not only need core programming and software, you also need a firewall, virus protection, and the power to delete files that are harmful to your system – a system maintenance schedule.

Virus protection is akin to inoculating yourself against outside attacks; your firewall prevents the 'hackers' from getting into your brain in the first place, and the delete option is your ability to cleanse your system of unwanted, unhelpful or otherwise damaging 'software' that others have planted in your mind. Let's explore some psychological tools that you can use to build up your own protection from external attack.

## Strengthen Your 'Core Programming'

Maggie Thatcher, later Lady Margaret Thatcher, was an excellent role model for what's called 'Internal Referencing'. In simple terms internal referencing is about the degree to which you place importance in what *you* think compared with what *other people* think. It's about confidence in your own convictions in the face of opposition; it's about feeling comfortable in taking a contrary position and standing your ground in the face of conflict.

Lady Thatcher most clearly demonstrated this character strength during her premiership when she was outvoted 49 to 1 in a European debate. On being quizzed afterwards by an interviewer about how she felt being the only person who voted against a proposal that everyone else had supported, her reply was... "I feel sorry for the other 49."

Now that is a strongly internally referenced response. Maggie certainly was a
powerful force to be reckoned with, after all she proclaimed at the same time:

> "You turn if you want to; The Lady's NOT for turning!"
>
> Margaret Thatcher

Okay, we can't all develop this strength of character or bravado overnight,
and Thatcher was clearly an extreme example, so what can we take of
practical use from this concept?

What internal referencing tells us is that a large proportion of any
confrontation is attitudinal. It's about not being prepared to be cowed by
others, not keeling over at the first hint of criticism, and it's about simply
deciding that no matter what someone else says or does, you are still a
worthwhile and valuable person.

You need to find the words that effectively sum this concept up for you; they
have to be your own. Attitudes and inner confidence cannot be learned from a
book, they have to be developed, and we've just said that you are the Master
Programmer of your own mind, so start from a solid base by making sure
you've got the right programmes installed in the first place.

| Tactic:  | Build your own sense of 'Internal Referencing' to form and strengthen your own opinion about what is right and wrong, what is, and what is not the case? |
| --- | --- |

Another useful way of thinking about this, which we referred to earlier, is to
simply recognise such jibes as a primitive form of attack, and to see them as
one of the lowest forms of intelligence. As such they just metaphorically slide
off you like oil off Teflon™... like water off a duck's back.

A person who resorts to throwing 'sticks and stones' at you has to be pretty desperate, insecure, unsophisticated or in some other disempowering position; in which case they're probably not worth fighting with.

I'm reminded of a friend many years ago, who found himself sitting in his BMW at a red traffic light when a car of more modest means, but which had clearly been performance-tuned, pulled alongside. As my friend waited for the lights to change, the lads in the other car were looking at him whilst the driver of the super-charged hot rod revved the engine in a baiting manner as if to say... 'Come on BMW Boy, we'll race you!' As the lights changed the other car screamed away, leaving skid marks on the tarmac. The driver accelerated across the junction at a completely unnecessary and clearly unsustainable speed, as the slow traffic on the other side of the junction meant that he would have to brake violently within seconds. Meanwhile, my friend slipped his car into first gear and pulled away from the lights effortlessly in an understated manner that silently said "I've got nothing to prove in this situation, least of all, to you'. He could have added "...whoever you aren't?"

Who's in control?

In that instant my friend had refused to be baited, and in so doing he automatically raised himself above the childish, boorish behaviour of his anonymous taunters. It seems to me that yet again, the provocateurs had proven the rule that the more you try to pretend to be something that you're not, the more you expose yourself for being the exact opposite. If you feel you have to prove something to someone else then it's not only a sign of your own insecurity, it's also a sign of your inadequacy in that which you profess to be.

So one of the first practical things you can do is to question why you should lower yourself to another person's level of behaviour. Why should you even allow another person to contaminate you or your thinking in any way? Are you so devoid of self-respect or self-control that you allow yourself to be dragged down to fighting in the gutter with such people?

##  Health Warning

I'm being deliberately provocative in my choice of words here in order to make the point, and to illustrate the broader philosophy behind this psychological technique which can be summarised as:

---

**Tactic:**  Mentally rise above the 'gutter rats', refusing to be dragged down to their level.

---

As Oscar Wilde once remarked:

*"We are all of us in the gutter, but some of us are looking at the stars".*

Oscar Wilde

More specifically, here's another wonderful quote which I am often reminded of when faced with situations where I could so easily have been dragged into a fight, whether verbal or physical:

*"When you fight with a pig you both get dirty...*

*...but the pig enjoys it!"*

Unknown

Keep this simple philosophy at the front of your mind as it can be just what you need the next time you're tempted to get dragged into a dirty squabble!

Now here's a touch of extra 'magic'.

## 'Mona Lisa' Technique

You can go further than simply refusing to be drawn into a situation; you can actually turn a potential irritator into a positive psychological advantage for you, if you use what I call the 'Mona Lisa' technique!

If you visit the Louvre in Paris you will see the surprisingly tiny painting 'Mona Lisa' smiling quietly to herself, unperturbed by the incessant crowds surrounding her. Let me explain the link by way of an example.

Imagine that a person is angry with you for some reason. This will be clear from their verbal and non-verbal behaviours; what they're saying, the manner in which they're saying it and from their body language. Remember, they have inherited these tell-tale behaviours from their prehistoric ancestors as part of the 'fight or flight' response.

By communicating in this way they're not only demonstrating their anger towards you at a conscious level, but they're also unintentionally revealing that they're not fully in control. This gives you a clue as to how you could respond.

The key with the Mona Lisa technique is to focus your attention on how the **other person** is behaving and feeling. What most people do when faced with such a situation however is to become consumed with how they are feeling themselves, and hence they are likely to become defensive or argumentative in return.

With the Mona Lisa technique you reverse the focus of your thinking, which is counter-intuitive; and that's exactly why it works. As most people normally respond with emotion, defensiveness or anger, then responding with none of these reactions is highly unusual, and unsettling to the provocateur.

Often in warfare or other conflict situations the key to success is to act or react in a way in which the opponent least expects; if you want to learn more then read about Tsun Tsu, a leading Chinese exponent of such ancient wartime strategies. The Mona Lisa technique is not an aggressive act, but it does give you an edge, precisely because it's unexpected.

Now, smiling quietly to oneself may sound a bit smug, and I'm not advocating that you physically smile; I'm simply using this as a metaphor. However it sums up the technique nicely as it goes beyond mere mantras such as... "No matter what you say or do you cannot damage me by words alone". It takes it to the next level, which effectively says... "And the more you try to do so, the more it exposes you for the weak and unsophisticated creature that you are. The more you try to resort to these child-like tactics the more stupid it just makes you look".

Effectively, through your lack of saying anything out loud you *are* saying something to them. It's a case of what you don't say, rather than what you do say, and what you're really communicating is... "Is that **really** the very best that you can do?"

Silence is golden, and strategic silence can be particularly powerful.

---

**Tactic:**        Use the 'Mona Lisa' technique: Smile quietly to yourself

---

  **Health Warning**

I am using a metaphor of the Mona Lisa in order to convey the essence of a technique. I am <u>not</u> suggesting that you actually practise smiling quietly to yourself in front of a mirror. If you're caught doing that then people really will start to wonder about you, and the consequences may be rather different! Nor am I advocating that you use childish, sarcastic expressions such as "Pull the other one, it's got bells on!" You're likely to get thumped.

This is simply an example of a label that I've chosen to apply to an intangible mental strategy so that we can begin to develop a common language. Many of these techniques are not written down anywhere; I'm trying to extend the catalogue of unlabelled human psychological tricks and gambits, and to make these available to a wider audience; to do that we need a shared language.

So, Mona Lisa is simply a label for 'standing back' from the emotion of a situation. More specifically it means that you:

1. Ignore how you are feeling and reacting (at least temporarily)

2. Focus upon how the other person is succeeding in getting themselves worked up into an unhelpful state, be that irritation, anger, annoyance, frustration or some other unstable position?

3. Let them get on with it!

From a purely sadistic perspective this is a great way to have fun whilst watching someone else increase in frustration. However, like many of the techniques I suggest in this book it comes with a strong 'Health Warning' which means that it needs to be used judiciously. Anything that's likely to provoke another person is potentially dangerous and so should be used with care. However, life is not fair, and so if people approach you with an intention to unnerve or upset you then it's only right that you're fully equipped with a comprehensive range of tools with which to respond.

In summary then, your first level of personal protection is to clean up your internal programming i.e. how you think about things. However, in many cases it's not enough to simply remain passive; we need to be more proactive. So, let's now invest in a 'personal firewall' to actively keep out the nasty stuff, the cerebral criminals, the mental muggers and the 'human hackers' who seek to bugger with our brains.

## Strengthen Your Personal 'Firewall'

Assuming your internal programming is okay, the second layer of defence is your personal firewall. In human, rather than computer terms you can think of this as developing a 'thicker skin'.

Your physical skin is a protective layer; it keeps your body parts neatly contained and in place and is your first line of defence to outside elements. However, human skin is not like an impenetrable steel wall, it's permeable, letting liquids and gases both in and out, for very good reason, and it can easily be damaged.

The previous techniques of Internal Referencing and not allowing yourself to get dragged down into quibbles, quarrels and arguments are attitudinal in nature. However, a personal firewall is more of an active and dynamic defence shield that lets some things in whilst actively repelling others; so, the techniques described here are of a more practical and tangible nature. The first of which is about developing a sense of curiosity about what people say and how they behave , and then in choosing your intellectual and emotional response to each and every situation.

| | |
|---|---|
| **Tactic:**  | Refuse to take everything at face value. Develop an attitude of 'curiosity' about what other people say and the opinions that they hold. |

In practice, the way in which you would do this is through a range of verbal responses. Here are some of my favourites:

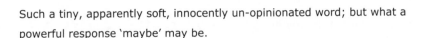

Tactic: Use the power of the word "Maybe".

Such a tiny, apparently soft, innocently un-opinionated word; but what a powerful response 'maybe' may be.

Anyone who has brought up young children will be familiar with constant requests for sweets, trips out, favours and other treats. Parental responses of "Yes" or "No" are obvious choices and in many cases they're entirely appropriate. However, these are like black and white, night and day or on and off; there is no middle ground or room for doubt, no hint of grey, possibility or negotiation.

A "No" response is likely to provoke negative reactions from the child ranging from withdrawal and sulks to tantrums, foot stomping, door banging or screaming at the supermarket checkout

A "Yes" on the other hand, is much easier to deliver. However, constantly agreeing to demands from a child can have longer-term consequences, not least on your pocket.

More damagingly, by always saying "Yes" you're potentially setting damaging expectations as the child will believe that they will always get what they want. You're also positioning yourself as an easy touch or a softie who can be relied upon to give in to whatever's requested. Equally, if you always say "No" then you're probably not being reasonable, and there are likely to be more serious long-term consequences for your relationship.

So let's get back to "maybe". Consider the power of the word; how do you think these five letters might change the dynamics of a situation?

"Maybe" implies possibility without categorically saying "Yes" or "No"; because it's non-committal, it leaves the subject open to debate.

Assuming that the other person genuinely wants what they're asking for, it heightens their attention and focuses them upon how they can persuade you to tip your response in favour of a "Yes". They're likely to remain engaged and to want to work *with* you; not a bad position from which to proceed.

This is the use of 'maybe' in response to a specific request; though in these situations you're usually already in a position of power, as someone's asking you for something. However, 'maybe' has a far more powerful use in situations that are less clear-cut, or in which there is a degree of controversy or tension. In particular you can use 'maybe' in order to respond to another person's stated opinion, without either agreeing or causing an argument – at least not initially.

For example:

Provocateur 1:    *"I think that you need to get over your need to have 'air time' with each of the senior managers in this organisation."*

Response 1:     *"Maybe.*
                *There could be something in what you say? However, I think there are more complicated things going on here."*

Provocateur 2:    *"If you say that to him he'll shoot you down in flames."*

Response 2:     *"'Maybe... or maybe not. That's a risk I'm prepared to take."*

In addition to 'maybe', there are other words or short expressions that you can use to achieve a similar outcome, including:

- "Could be."

- "Possibly."

- "That's interesting."

- "I can see why you might think that." ... etc.

Regardless of the words you choose (and you will think of many more), the intention of the technique remains the same; to avoid giving a categorical answer to a direct provocation, at least not initially.

By side-stepping the direct, definitive answer, you achieve several things at once:

1. You avoid a direct confrontation, which prevents an argument
2. You keep several options open, which gives you flexibility
3. You highlight the fact that you remain to be convinced, which keeps the pressure on the other party to make the next move

All this from just one, apparently innocuous word?

You're now beginning to appreciate the potent power of the magic contained within our language.

As with many things that are worthwhile learning, you'll need to practise this linguistic technique. You need to get yourself to the point where you do this instinctively rather than having to consciously apply it whenever you remember. I say this to prepare you for Chapter Seven, where we will really get our 'magician's cloak' on, and potently dispel, or 'dis-spell' the curses of others.

Before we move on though, here's another 'diffuser' word with a subtle, yet powerful message, and that's the word 'Potentially.'

> **Tactic**      Use the power of the word "Potentially".
>

'Potentially' is a great word.

It indicates that what has just been said by another person *may* be right in *principle*, whilst at the same time cunningly indicating that it's unlikely to be the case in *practice*.

'Potentially' refers to something having the capability or potential to be or to achieve something, which is very different from it actually delivering on its promise. Having the potential to deliver, and actually delivering are not the same thing.

We can all potentially use 100% of our brains, but medical scientists and psychologists tell us that we only use a fraction of our potential brain power at any one time. The able-bodied majority can potentially walk across every continent on Earth on foot, given enough time, resources, stamina, determination or whatever, but how many people actually do?

So 'potentially' implies nothing more than capability, and when you use it in response to someone else's claim you're not only avoiding direct disagreement, you're simultaneously, and more powerfully, casting doubt upon whether this is, or will ever be the case.

Some examples will help illustrate:

Provocateur 3:     *"If you put that in now it will get damaged."*

Response 3:       "Potentially; though I guess we won't know until we try."

This response is dismissive of the likelihood that damage will occur in practice, and indicates that you are going to do it anyway.

Provocateur 4:     *"They could send you to prison for that."*

Response 4:     "Potentially; but they'd have to catch me first."

Again, this response indicates that it's not beyond the bounds of possibility, but they probably won't get sent to jail, and even before that point there's another hurdle to get over which is the unlikely chance of being discovered in the first place.

Let's pause for a moment, in case you're thinking that this is getting too linguistically anal.

Maybe it is...                    ... you see I can't help myself.

'Maybe' aside, my point is that there's a huge amount of nuance and subtlety within our day-to-day English language, and the vast majority of people don't recognise how much meaning and influence is hidden within the words that we use; at least not at a conscious level. Consequently, because it's not part of our normal conscious awareness, it's easy to initially dismiss these subtleties as unimportant. Believe me, they are not.

Some people describe this phenomenon as 'Not knowing what I don't know'; a concept most clumsily described by Donald Rumsfeld in an infamous US news briefing in 2002.

*"As we know, there are known knowns; things that we know we know.*

*We also know there are known unknowns;*

*That is to say, we know there are some things we don't know.*

> *But there are also unknown unknowns;*
>
> *The ones we don't know we don't know."*

Feb. 12, 2002, Department of Defence news briefing

Putting obvious examples aside, the nuances and subtleties of our language *are* picked up by listeners, but crucially, and this is the key to subtle and artful influence, *this happens almost always at an unconscious level.*

You will not have noticed the majority of these, precisely because they were unconscious. By way of example, did anything that you read in the last minute leave a 'nasty taste' in your mouth? If so, then you will know what I mean, at a conscious level. However it's just possible that your unconscious mind processed the words and left you feeling a little uneasy, or queasy, without fully understanding why.

So, some messages are like Trojan Horses that are subtly installed into another person's mind, and it's specifically *because* their installation goes largely undetected that they're so powerful. The most dangerous type of human 'killer' is the one that you don't even know is already hiding in your house. So too with killer words and phrases.

Here are some more every-day examples to illustrate:

Person 1:    *"I don't want you to feel too guilty about missing your appointment."*

Sub-text:    You are/should be feeling guilty that you missed an appointment.

Person 2:    [On the telephone] *"Before you hang up, could you just ..."*

Sub-text:     You're going to hang up the phone in a moment/this telephone conversation is coming to an end.

This is actually what's called a 'hidden command' i.e. I am telling you to do something without having to tell you to do it.

Person 3:     *"I'm conscious that you're very busy…"*

Sub-text:     I'm not going to waste too much of my time dealing with this/you.

Person 4:     *"When do you plan to give your wife a break from the housework?"*

Sub-text:     You're going to give her a break/you should/you have to give her a break some time soon; the only thing to be discussed is precisely when you will do it?

Are we getting too deep into semantics, or merely getting up to some antics?

I don't think either apply; I could go on with literally hundreds of ways in which statements or questions can be phrased in order to influence at a subconscious level, but that's not the main purpose of the book. For now, all I want to do is to help you to appreciate the power of such 'subliminal' expressions, because we will return to this subject several times as you read further.

Now here's a quick test. What were the two subliminal commands that I used in the last sentence above, beginning in… 'For now', and ending in 'further'? See if you can spot them before you read the answers below.

Answers:  1. Subliminal expressions are powerful
2. You are going to carry on reading

So, now that you're beginning to realise that these distinctions are indeed powerful, and that they work in practice, you need to prove this to yourself by trying them out and noticing the results you get.

Let's now remind ourselves of the key tactic that encompasses our linguistic response to provocative assertions.

| | |
|---|---|
| **Tactic:**  | Use 'diffuser' words when you want to avoid giving a categorical answer to a direct provocation, when you want to avoid direct confrontation, when you wish to keep your options open, or when you want to highlight that you remain to be convinced. |

In summary then, we've recognised that any firewall has the potential to be penetrated, and to be effective we need to learn when to reject known threats and when to allow other things through.

The stage of the game that we're at right now is to raise our conscious awareness of the subliminal power of the words that people use and the statements they make, and to recognise these for what they are.

The good news is that the more we raise our conscious awareness in this area, and the stronger we build our firewall, the more we will be able to prevent mere words from harming us. We have not given them permission to enter, and so no matter how 'cutting' the remarks may seem, our defences have already become more of a match for them. We're building up systemic resistance.

## Back to You

Getting your core programming up to excellent health, and stopping the 'nasties' from getting in is only part of your personal defence mechanism. As with a computer, things will occasionally get through, and so you need to be ready to deal with any viruses that manage to penetrate.

We will be dealing with this topic throughout the rest of this book, and so as a start let's take a look at some of the milder forms of viruses, the things that irritate and agitate us as part of everyday life, and examine some more practical and quick ways of dealing with these.

# Chapter 5

Options, Choices, Control & Thinking

# 5
# Options, Choices, Control & Thinking

## The Power of Multiple Options

Henry Ford famously said… "You can have any colour as long as it's black."

I, rather less famously said… "When you have one choice in life you have no choice; because one option is no option at all."

Think about it.

Stress often results from a situation in which you feel trapped, constrained, hapless, helpless and hopeless. If you have no say in how things will turn out, or any alternative courses of action open to you, then this often results in negative stress and pressure.

Given an element of choice however, and you start to regain a sense of control over your own destiny. Choice is empowering because being able to make a personal decision about something puts you in the driving seat; it puts you in control. Rather than hapless, helpless and hopeless, you're composed, capable and confident.

Interestingly, even if the decision you take is to *not* take an alternative option, for example you choose to turn down a job offer from another company, you still retain an element of control as it is *you* who has made the decision to stay with your current employer. You had the choice, you weighed up two alternatives and made your decision accordingly; you were in control. So, in any situation, the person who has more options is generally the one with more control over that situation; and with increased control comes increased power.

---

**Provocation**

The person with the most options available to them is the one with the most control in any situation.

Increased options equate with increased confidence, greater power and a higher level of control.

---

Suppose, for example, you're selling your car and your only potential buyer is offering to take the car right now for cash, but she's offering you 10% less than the asking price. If you absolutely have to sell the car today and there is no prospect of another buyer showing up that afternoon, then there's a strong chance that you'll accept her offer. You will resent the sale, resent the buyer, resent having to give in to a raw deal and you'll reluctantly bank the money.

If, on the other hand, you have appointments with other interested buyers later that day (even though they are yet to make you an offer, if at all), you have the option to say "No" to your present buyer and to push for a higher price. This is because you know that you do not have to concede right there and then. You can walk away, even if only temporarily... but remember to take the keys with you! You have potential options, you have potential choice, you have more control, you retain the upper hand... and a healthier bank balance as a result... potentially.

So, it's generally a good thing in life to have, 'Possibilities, Options, Choices and Alternatives'; I call these your 'POCA's'. As in a game of poker, the person with the best hand (the widest range and number of POCA's), controls the game.

So, the more POCA's you have, *or can generate* in any situation, the less pressured you will feel to make a rash or rushed decision, and the less stress you will feel. You'll also come out 'winning' more than 'losing', or at least you won't be left feeling that you've been duped, arm-twisted, manipulated, harangued, forced, cheated or deceived... again!

Okay, it's all very well saying 'Have more options'; but how do you generate more options if right now you feel as though all you have is 'Hobson's Choice' i.e. no choice at all?

Of course every situation is contextual so it's not possible to give anything other than generic advice here. You have to actively look for and explore alternative options, create them yourself, explore different courses of action ahead of time (so that you don't feel pressured to do this in the thick of a situation such as the one described above), and you need to think 'out of the box'.

Some call it 'contingency planning' i.e.

> "What do I do if I don't get my way on this one?"

> "What if it all goes 'belly up'?"

> "What do I do as a fallback option?"

As Dale Carnegie said... *"If I'm handed a lemon, how can I turn it into lemonade?"*

Just asking yourself questions such as these, in advance, should be enough to kick-start your thinking.

> **Tactic:** Always have at least one alternative course of action
>  available to you. If you haven't a 'Plan B', then find or create
> one before you find yourself in the situation of having to
> choose between 'Plan A' and nothing.

## Much Ado About Nothing

When looked at in relative terms things often assume new meaning, and the viewer gains a fresh, more helpful and empowering perspective on an issue, problem or opportunity.

The £15 you saved by taking your kids to McDonalds rather than the local Bistro pales into insignificance when compared to the £5,000 bonus you missed at work this year, or the extra £200 per month that you're paying for the next three years as a consequence of fixing your mortgage rate at the 'wrong' time.

The anger you felt over dropping that bottle of gin in the supermarket car park last week is nothing compared to the £300 a month depreciation your car is suffering as it sits on your driveway. You would have to smash a bottle of gin every day of the year just to equal that degree of continuous and unrelenting vehicular loss. Now, smashing gin bottles on a daily basis *would* be stupid, yet how stupid is it to get more angry over a £10 bottle of cheap spirit than about losing £300 depreciation on your car every month?

The insult you felt, and still feel, as a result of being shown two fingers by a motorist this morning (who, by the way, you don't even know, don't want to know and will never meet again), is nothing compared to the love expressed to you by your partner or close family member when you get home that evening. Yet do you expend the same degree of positive appreciative emotion in response to them as you did in reacting negatively and angrily towards that abusive asshole of a driver? See, even I'm getting emotive, and I wasn't even in your car!

What's more important to you?

- Getting that report on your boss' desk by 5pm today, or dropping everything to attend to your child who's just been taken ill at school?

- Saving a few quid in the pub by ensuring that you don't arrive at the bar first, and leaving just before it's your round, or being generous with both time and money, and in so doing building close trusting relationships with your friends?

The point I'm making is that we all need to get, and keep things in perspective. It's vital to put things into their proper context. In the 'grand scheme of things' many daily irritations, losses and frustrations will simply pale into insignificance against the broader backdrop of all the other, far more important things going on in your life.

The challenge is in being able to lift yourself out of the detail, which often also means rising above the emotion of a situation, in order to see a bigger, more complete, more relevant and important picture. If, despite this new perspective, the previous issue still figures prominently, then there are many things that you can do to deal with it which we will cover later; the point here is:

| | |
|---|---|
| **Tactic:**  | Get things in proportion; put them into their proper context and perspective... and keep them there. |

In Chapter Ten I will show you a psychological technique to do this, but we're not ready for that one just yet; we've more work to do first.

We discussed earlier how stress can often result from a lack of perceived control in one's life. Stress arises when we blow things out of proportion, make a bigger deal of something than it truly deserves, focus on the wrong things or find ourselves spending a disproportionate amount of time focusing on small matters; a behaviour I call 'Majoring in Minors'.

Let's take a typical family problem. The kids won't tidy their bedrooms, the rooms are in a constant mess with clothes left on the floor (the 'floordrobe'), drawers hanging out and with barely a square inch of carpet visible beneath piles of 'stuff' that hasn't been put away. You're fed up with getting angry over the state of their rooms, which you usually end up tidying yourself in a fit of frustration and rage. What compounds your irritation is the fact that this has been going on for several years now, without any sign of improvement.

So, yet again you go upstairs to find the kids' bedrooms looking like a scene from a war zone.

What alternatives do you now have?

What's your first, natural normal reaction in this situation?

1. Scream and shout at them again, just like you've been doing for as long as you remember. You know this technique has not worked in the past though you continue to use it; which is interesting in itself.

2. Tell them that if they clean up their rooms then you will reward them with a treat such as a visit to the cinema. You know that this approach hardly

ever works either, yet somehow it's worth a try, and it feels better than screaming and getting angry.

3. Offer to pay them £5 each to tidy their rooms – a 'carrot' approach. Now you're moving onto dodgy ground. Isn't it their responsibility anyway, or do you now need to be paying your kids to flush the toilet after them, eat their meals and to comb their hair before going to school? Also, over-use of this approach will mean that you're flat broke by the end of the month.

4. Tell them that if they don't clean up their rooms then you will impose some form of punishment such as refusing to let them have their friends round for a sleepover at the weekend - the 'stick' approach. Again, past experience has taught you that this technique only ever results in stubbornness, arguments, bad feelings on both sides and a stalemate. What's more, it usually ends with you giving in, as barring their friends from the house would be punishing their mates as well, would create more enemies for yourself, would label you as a bad parent and saddle you with the self-imposed guilt and shame that accompanies this. Even so, you try the threatened punishment ploy regardless; you're grasping at straws.

5. Go upstairs and tidy their rooms yourself, often accompanied by a lot of noise and stomping around as you audibly try to make the point that you're doing this in protest, and it's they who should be tidying their own rooms. Note: you achieve the objective of having tidy kids' bedrooms, at least temporarily; however, it was at your expense in terms of your time, your energy and your frayed emotions. More fundamentally you've taught your kids that if they leave their rooms messy for long enough you will cave in and do their job for them; smart move huh?

So, that's five well known strategies that, in the past, have been proven to be highly reliable. Reliable in the sense that you can have a high degree of confidence that they will end in failure, and to make things even worse, you will end up feeling bad at some point in the process – a double whammy!

So, what alternatives do you have? Remember, with alternatives comes choice, control and power.

The simplest way to illustrate this tactic is by means of a ridiculous Doctor/Patient scenario:

Patient:     *"Doctor, doctor."*

Doctor:     "Yes, how can I help?"

Patient:     *"It hurts whenever I reach my left arm over my left shoulder, bend it around the back of my head and grab hold of my nose from the other side."*

Doctor:     "Well don't do it then."

Patient:     *"Okay, I'll try that. Thanks doctor."*

One of the principles that I want to impress upon you is....

If what you have done, or are continuing to do, is not working i.e. it's not giving you the results you desire, then *try something else*, almost *anything* else, but *something* else, because what you have repeatedly done in the past is clearly not working.

Now I know this sounds like common sense logic, and you don't need to buy a book to tell you that. However, how often do you see people trapped in recurring patterns of behaviour, which predictably end up with them not getting the results that they want, yet they keep pushing ahead regardless? Perhaps you need to lend them this book after you've finished reading it.

So, rather than persisting in pushing at the same 'locked door', or continually jiggling the wrong 'key' in the lock, try stepping back mentally from the situation and ask yourself what alternatives you could try?

Taking the metaphorical locked door as an example, how about:

· Waiting for the door to open from the inside

· Trying a number of different keys

· Knocking on the door and asking if you can come in

· Asking when would be the best time to return?

· Pulling the door rather that pushing it - perhaps it wasn't locked after all, it just opens forwards

· Smashing it open with a sledge hammer (probably not a long-term viable solution)

· Examining it to see if you can loosen the hinges and get in that way

· Walking away and trying a different door

· Building your own door... etc

Metaphors aside, the point to remember is that if what you're doing isn't working then you have to try something else, almost anything else, just something else, because what you're currently doing is patently not working.

You have nothing to lose, and potentially a lot to gain.

| | |
|---|---|
| **Tactic:**  | If what you are doing is not working then try something else, *anything* else, just so long as it's *something* else. |

## Sixth Sense

So, back to our messy bedroom scenario, what sixth strategy could you apply that might make sense?

One way of thinking about this is to think in opposites. Here's an old joke to illustrate:

Q. *"How do you keep flies out of the kitchen?"*

A. "Put a bucket of manure in the lounge!"

The joke, and solution, relies upon a reversal in thinking. Instead of thinking of ways in which to keep flies *out of the kitchen* we think of ways to *divert the flies elsewhere*, and silly as it sounds, the technique works. Try it for yourself; if you live alone, and don't mind living alone for the rest of your life, that is!

So, rather than thinking of ways in which we can get a child's bedroom tidy, what would happen if we were to reverse our thinking and instead consider ways in which it could become messier?

If you follow this line of thinking it won't be long before you come up with the suggestion of leaving the rooms as they are, walking away and just letting the kids get on with it. The practical step you take would be to close their bedroom doors and re-direct your energy towards getting the rest of the house into presentable condition.

I once had a neighbour who spent some considerable time working out how to wallpaper behind their radiators; clearly a tricky operation. She had tried pushing the pre-pasted paper down behind the panels using a ruler, a hard-backed book, a tea tray and an assortment of other long thin implements. She had tried feeding the paper up from below and slipping her hand down from above to try to grab the soggy paper, or using BBQ tongs to catch hold of it and pull it up; quite creative really. When the paper kept tearing or getting stuck she finally decided to try to unhook a radiator from the wall (whilst it was still plumbed in), and stick the wallpaper behind the panel whilst balancing the full radiator on top of her thighs.

As a consequence, the radiator slipped, the soft copper pipe ruptured and a few gallons of hot water poured from the central heating system onto the lounge carpet. Imagine my neighbour's unexpected pleasure as she knelt alone under the lounge window, bathing her thighs in warm, pulsating dirty water, whilst grappling with a radiator and a ream of sticky wallpaper!

Now, the good thing about her actions is she was exploring POCA's (see earlier), she was being resourceful in ensuring that she was not confined by just one option. The stupid thing about my neighbour's behaviour, however, was that she hadn't realised that nobody would be able to see that far down behind the back of a radiator in any case, let alone be remotely interested in doing so, and so the task was itself completely pointless! This is another example of where 'not taking action' i.e. the equivalent of shutting the door on the untidy bedrooms, can actually be a good policy.

Now, don't think for a moment that shutting the door on a messy bedroom is a weak admission of failure or giving in too soon. Of course, if this is how you *always* respond then it's not a strategy, it really is a weak running away response, and an example of how not to apply the principle of trying something different. If you always run away from situations like this, then you're guilty of sticking too rigidly to another fixed pattern of unhelpful behaviour – something we discussed in Chapter Two.

So, how else might shutting the door on the mess be interpreted, and how might it actually be a constructive, helpful strategy in this case?

One interpretation is that you've decided that you're no longer going to allow your children to dictate how you feel about certain things. You have come to the conclusion that their rooms are already a mess, so how much more messy would it be possible for them to become? Not much is my guess. You reason that pretty soon, when they realise that mum or dad are not going to do their predictable, manic running around tidying up act, that it will occur to them that when they can't find any of their things it's not in their own interests to live in a hovel. For you, in addition to freeing up a couple of hour's cleaning and tidying from your weekly routine, you're also increasingly gaining mental control. Even more significantly, you're developing the maturity of your children as they learn to take more personal responsibility, and have greater self-respect for their things, their home and their environment... and in you.

So, by considering a seemingly counter-intuitive strategy such as 'shutting the door on the mess' in these terms, it becomes a powerful, legitimate and beneficial response, at least in this case.

---

**Tactic:**    Consider doing the opposite of what the situation seems to demand, even if this at first appears to be counter-intuitive.

You don't need to act on your thinking; the process of looking at a situation in this way is likely to throw up more possibilities, options, choices and alternatives (POCA's).

---

POCA's give you choice, options and control.

## Is a Child About to Die?

I don't mean to upset anyone with this provocative question, though I would add that my wife and I lost a daughter soon after her birth, so we can at least appreciate, from first hand, the immense power of such a question.

Hopefully few readers will be able to identify with this from first hand experience, however, the provocative question... 'Is a child about to die?' is capable of immediately and abruptly changing how a person is thinking about a situation. What's more, you can use this one on yourself!

Sometimes people get themselves worked up needlessly over issues and problems; issues that are either trivial in themselves, or potential problems that are so unlikely to happen that the amount of fuss the person's making is unwarranted.

My mother, for example, is terrified of dying in a plane crash. She retains this fear even though I've pointed out to her that statistically she has more chance of being kicked to death by a donkey – and she doesn't lie awake at night worrying about donkeys!

So, the next time you come across someone stressing about something, and you can see that in the grand scheme of things they're getting it all out of proportion, try asking... "Excuse me, but is a child about to die?", and note the reaction you get. They'll often stop in their tracks, smile, look puzzled, or laugh. Nine times out of ten they will re-appraise the situation in a more realistic light. If nothing else, the question immediately breaks their negative self-reinforcing thought pattern, enabling them to consider the situation in a different way.

It's a general rule that any question begs an answer, even if the answer is only conjured up in the mind of the listener and is not outwardly verbalised. In order to understand what has been asked, the listener has to answer the question in their own head first. When we seek to influence another person with questions, we do not always need them to answer our questions out loud; we just need them to do this within the confines of their own mind.

By the way, I was just wondering what your biggest personal secret is?

No, you don't have to tell me, but you know what it is don't you; and I've just reminded you of something that I don't even know about myself.

Consider what you do mentally when someone asks you... "What did you do at the weekend?" Your immediate reaction is unlikely to be "What business is that of yours, you nosey bastard?" The question automatically directs your thoughts to what you actually did do at the weekend. Similarly, if you're sitting with a friend in a bar and they gesture towards another person saying... "I can't help wondering what s(he) would look like naked", I challenge you NOT to immediately imagine that person without any clothes on! Even as you're reading this an image of a naked person flashed into your mind; it did didn't it? Go on admit it!

I wonder what's in your fridge at home...?

Now back to the technique characterised by the more serious question "Is a child about to die?" Clearly, we hope that the immediate answer to the question is "No, a child's life is not at risk here." However, and far more importantly, from this altered perspective you can move them forward in a new direction - you've successfully broken their thought pattern.

Your intention in all of this is to help the other person to move to a more constructive pattern of thinking, but you cannot do this gently. In order to break people out of powerfully damaging, destructive thought patterns such as these we often have to do it dramatically - hence the provocative nature of this, or similar questions.

> *"Will this lead to the outbreak of war?"*
>
> *"Does this mean the end of civilization as we know it?"*

"Shall I just kill you now, and put you out of this abject misery?"

Of course this technique works just as effectively when you use it on yourself. Next time you find yourself in a difficult situation ask yourself... "Now wait a moment, are we talking about a child's life, or my own life being in danger here? Clearly not, so what exactly *are* we talking about. What exactly is it that's worth me getting so worked up about?"

These linguistic techniques will enable you to gain a more balanced personal perspective. They're especially useful when you find yourself dealing with a difficult situation on your own, with no-one else around to give you this refreshing and helpful perspective on the world.

| Tactic:  | Question:  "Is a child about to die?" <br> - or another similarly ridiculous apocalyptic question. |
|---|---|

So, what *is* in your fridge right now?

## What's the Worst that Could Possibly Happen?

Okay, let's imagine that a child's life really *is* in danger, or you're clinging onto a window ledge of a burning building, 30 feet off the ground, with no obvious option other than to jump. What do you do right now?

We can take some inspiration and advice from Dale Carnegie, the famous human relations guru from the 1930's, and author of the international bestseller 'How to Win Friends and Influence People'. In another of his books, 'How to Stop Worrying and Start Living', Carnegie gives us an extremely practical formula for dealing with difficult, or stressful issues and problems.

Carnegie bases this upon your self-analysis of the situation using three simple questions:

1. "What is the worst that could happen if I can't solve this problem?"
2. "Am I prepared to accept the worst if I can't solve it?"
3. "What can I do now to prevent the worst happening or to lessen its impact should it occur?"

When you're trapped on a ledge of a burning building it's probably safe to assume that you will have 100% focus on your present predicament! You will quickly assess your situation, your options and the actions you can take.

If you have no option other than to jump, and to jump right now, then you will be focused upon the likely consequences of jumping in terms of personal injuries. Assuming that you consider survival with a few broken bones to be a preferable outcome to death by being burnt alive, you will jump.

Having taken that decision (remember, you have now decided to jump so that is no longer in debate), your focus will then shift towards how you can lessen the impact of the fall. For example, reducing the distance between you and the impact point by hanging from your arms, aiming yourself towards as soft a landing as possible, or breaking the speed of your fall by using your jacket as a mini parachute etc.

Because you are already prepared to accept the worst (a few broken bones), then anything that you can do to prevent this happening, or to reduce the severity of bodily damage, has got to be beneficial. By using Carnegie's 3 step formula, and being prepared to accept the worst, then you are freed from worrying about this. You can instead devote all of your thinking power towards improving upon the worst and making the best of a thoroughly inconvenient situation. Often in life, that's exactly what we have to do; we have to make the very best we can, with what we have, right now, and from a bad situation.

*"It's happened – get over it!"* is an often used expression that recognises that history cannot be changed and we have to move on. However, it doesn't exactly help the individual to do so, particularly if the event has involved severed limbs, a marital breakup or some other highly traumatising incident, and there is little or no empathy from the speaker.

*"We are where we are"* is another well-intentioned statement that can be helpful in getting people to accept the situation they're in, and to think forward from that point in terms of improving things.

However, assuming the person is not yet in such dire circumstances, a useful question would be "If this *were* to happen, and you can't prevent it from happening, then what can you do right now to prepare for it, and to reduce the impact of its consequences?"

If it *has* already happened, then a whole new set of questions would need to be asked about what can be done right now to respond, re-group and recover.

So we now have another tool in our kit bag, courtesy of Dale Carnegie...

| | |
|---|---|
| **Tactic:** <br> 👍 | Use Dale Carnegie's 3-step problem solving approach: <br><br> 1. What's the worst that could happen if I can't solve this problem? <br><br> 2. Am I prepared to accept the worst if I can't solve it? <br><br> 3. What can I do right now to prevent the worst happening, or if it's inevitable, to lessen its impact? |

**Health Warning**

Before we leave this subject it's time for another 'Health Warning'.

Earlier in this chapter I used the title of one of Shakespeare's plays: 'Much Ado About Nothing'. I will therefore close with another; 'Romeo and Juliet'.

About a third of the way into the play, Mercutio, Romeo's best friend is engaged in a brawl with the town's bully, Tibalt. During the scrap Tibalt draws a knife and plunges it into Mercutio's tunic.

Alarmed, Romeo and his friends run over to see if Mercutio is hurt, to which Mercutio replies, whilst holding his side "Ah tis a scratch, a mere scratch. Nay tis not as wide as a church door nor as deep as a well, but 'twill suffice." In his characteristically joking manner Mercutio was making light of a fatal injury. His final utterance before he died was... "A curse on both your houses!"

So, not everything can be dismissed as none life-threatening, and if you look hard enough you will find exceptions to every rule*.

Returning to the point I made earlier, it's about gaining an appropriate perspective on each situation you face, about framing this within its proper context and in using some of the tools above to move forward in more positive and helpful ways.

---

* Except the rule that says 'there are exceptions to every rule', because by its very existence the rule disproves itself. Any exception to the 'there are exceptions to every rule' rule would indicate that there are occasions when there are no exceptions

# Chapter 6

## Get Your Thinking in Order

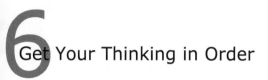

# 6 Get Your Thinking in Order

## If it Wasn't for 'Other People'

> *"Going abroad on holiday would be great...*
> *if it weren't for all the foreigners."*
>
> Anonymous

Have you ever gone on holiday or visited a popular tourist site and moaned about all the tourists? Have you ever become frustrated by being stuck in a traffic jam and found yourself cursing the volume of traffic?

Don't forget, you're not only on the receiving end of these problems...
*... you're part of the the problem in the first place!* After all, if you weren't in the traffic queue it would be fractionally shorter, thus making it marginally easier for the other drivers, and you wouldn't be pulling your hair out and cursing in the process. If you weren't populating the 'popular' tourist site it wouldn't be quite so popular, thus, paradoxically, making it marginally more attractive to visit. But then, as soon as you visit, that marginal attraction disappears!

One of the themes we will return to throughout this book is that our frustrations are not solely a result of other people's behaviours. We can be both part of the solution and party to the problem. There are two sides to the same 'coin'.

That said, many of our frustrations, disappointments, and conflicts do come from the actions of others. Yes, we curse because we can't get the shelves straight, a stiletto heel snaps on the way to work, or the broadband connection is playing up again, however these are all things that are pretty much within our control to fix. Yet notice how some people mutter and complain to inanimate objects, such as turning around and swearing at, or shaking a fist at a piece of broken pavement that they've just tripped over!

Technical and mechanical breakdowns aside, most of the more difficult and troublesome things that cause us problems on an ongoing basis are created by other people.

As a customer services assistant once said to me...

> *"If it wasn't for all these bloody customers*
> *we wouldn't have to deal with so many customer complaints!"*

So, short of taking yourself off to live alone on a deserted island (which technically speaking would then no longer be deserted), what can you do at a more practical level to control your level of irritation, frustration and anger with other people?

Notice I said, what can *you* do to control *your* level of irritation, not what can you do to sort out *other people*. This chapter is about practical tools and strategies that you can use within the privacy of your own mind.

### "Ooh... I Just Wish He Wouldn't Do That!"

Do you ever find yourself becoming irritated by something another person does, when in fact the consequences of their behaviour have absolutely no impact upon you whatsoever?

Think about it. How many times have you complained about something, and had a rant, when the subject in question had nothing to do with you and did not affect you in the slightest way? If you think you're immune from such apparently 'crazy' behaviour, just suspend your judgement for a moment because it happens more often than you might think.

For example, have you ever found yourself complaining about the price of an item that you have no intention of buying... "Look at the price of that; who'd pay that much for it, it's outrageous!" What about complaining about how other people dress... "What on Earth does *she* look like?" In the last case, by reversing your thinking (Chapter 5), you would realise that the poor clothing choices of others makes you look even more stylish, so, please celebrate other people's poor fashion choices from now on.

Think about it honestly; the guy next door who is perpetually washing his car, the woman who insists upon natural unassisted childbirth, the guy that slurps his soup, or the rail commuter who stands in exactly the same spot on the platform every day. What about the woman on the train who insists on sitting in the same seat every morning even though there are plenty of other vacant seats around the carriage? My wife even commented to me last night about a person being interviewed on the television; she said "Look, that man's head is too wobbly – it's so off-putting." She really was getting irritated by hi innocent and unconscious mannerisms.

These are tiny, potentially perplexing and inconceivably irritating aspects of other people's behaviour that can cause us to become annoyed. Forget the details of the examples above, the question is... do you find yourself becoming annoyed, irritated or disgruntled by the petty, ritualistic, and often un-thinking or unconscious actions of others?

That said, in the case of 'Mr.Wobblyhead', I was forced to agree with my wife. His side to side head movements were really off-putting, which meant that we spent most of our time watching his head wobbling from side to side, and commenting upon it, rather than listening to what he was saying. In fact we still can't remember the subject of the interview or the guy's name.

So you see, none of us are totally immune, not even me, and I'm writing a book about it!

(Editor's note: Doctor Lavelle, please take your own medicine.)

It seems to have become a national sport to discuss the eccentricities of other people's behaviour, be it in the playground waiting to pick up the kids, over the water-cooler in the office or as a social pastime of alcohol-fuelled dinner parties. As I stated in Chapter 1 there's been a plethora of books published in recent years that take disgruntlement and ranting to another level. Last week I read in the newspaper of a group of people who were thrown out of a pub in Wales for altering a menu board because they took offence at reading the word 'cake's'. Lynn Truss would have had a field day.

Today (writing of the 1$^{st}$ edition of this book) is September 15$^{th}$ 2007, and the BBC news is reporting mass panic from customers of the Northern Rock Building Society. Hundreds of people are queuing for hours to withdraw their money, as they fear that the Bank is about to collapse. There hasn't been a 'run' on a bank in the UK for 150 years.

Several high-minded commentators on the radio are criticising the 'small-minded', irrational behaviour of tens of thousands of people, in terms that barely stop short of calling them 'The Great Unwashed'. During a heated discussion in a radio phone-in programme, one caller was getting angry at the fact that so many people react like fools by panicking irrationally in such situations. He had taken the trouble to phone in, at his own expense in terms of call charges and time, to complain about a situation that did not affect him in any way whatsoever. He was neither a customer nor a shareholder of Northern Rock, and he had not personally witnessed or been inconvenienced by the queues at the bank. He was having a rant, and as a consequence was getting himself angry and worked up for no reason; he really was 'going off on one'.

By the time of publication of the first edition of this book (21st June 2008) the Northern Rock scenario had played itself out, and the Credit Crunch had left many more banks in trouble. However, my point is not about Northern Rock, but rather the behaviour of the telephone caller who was having a rant about something that did not in the slightest way concern him. He had not anticipated the indirect impact of the financial crisis that was about o unfold of course, his rant was about the 'sheep-like' behaviour of the queues of investors.

Sadly, this was also a dramatic example of how people, in seeking to avoid a problem actually make it worse, or precipitate the problem in the first place. If thousands had not simultaneously rushed to withdraw their money then maybe the bank would have survived?

Mass panic on the high street and telephone rants aside, there are numerous examples of idiosyncratic, harmless habits and rituals that people have developed, for whatever reason, rational or not. In many instances the individuals are not even aware of them, or if they are, they're using them as psychological 'comfort blankets'.

Remember of course, that from the perspective of other people, you are one of those 'other people' to them. The key is to accept that people are peculiar, individuals are individualistic, and none of their petty foibles, mannerisms, idiosyncrasies and behaviours should affect you in any way.

We all have our own personal favourite habit patterns and ways of getting through the day. What are yours, I wonder, and which of these do you think irritate other people the most?

Does your regular clearing of your throat annoy your colleagues, or bizarrely, have you ever considered that your eternally cheerful demeanour actually annoys your work mates? It's amazing how such little things can have the power to irritate some people. On the face of it why would anyone be irritated by someone's eternally cheery disposition? It sounds crazy, particularly as the alternative of a dour, po-faced grumble-monger would be much worse; yet it happens. I've even heard people saying things like "I'd really like to thump him, he's so bloody positive about everything", or "Ooh, I'd love to wipe that smile off her face."

Again, let me emphasise, my focus here is not upon the cheerful person, but rather upon the people around them who are allowing themselves to be narked, irritated or otherwise impacted in an unhelpful way. One more example might help illustrate this phenomenon.

Many readers will be familiar with the concept of 'Keeping up with the Jones'', in which it's easy to fall into the small-minded trap of comparing yourself with those around you, often in relation to the personal achievements and physical possessions of your colleagues, friends and neighbours. Whilst many of us are competitive by nature, if this spills over into more negative emotions such as jealousy, rivalry or bitterness, then we should take a step back and ask ourselves how such thoughts and feelings are helping us?

Generally they do not.

I once knew a guy who was obsessed by the fact that his neighbour of five years, whom he did not even know other than to say "Good morning" to, had a better car than him and was able to take his family on more luxurious holidays. He would often bring this up in conversation with me and it was clear that he had a chip on his shoulder about it.

Unfortunately, what had happened is that he had allowed himself to compare himself with, and get into a sort of one-sided competition with someone whom he hardly knew, and who was not important to him in any tangible way. He just happened to live next door to this 'random guy', but equally he could have found himself living next door to any one of several billion people. Was he going to compare himself with everyone on the planet? What about Mr. Rahim Ezzudin who lives at number 43 Jalal Bintan in Kuala Lumpur, who has a Mercedes and a small second home in Bali? What about Dan Schott, the computer engineer from Kansas who recently won $8m in the state lottery, whom my friend also does not know? Perhaps he should start making a list, because there are so many people out there that need competing with!

When looked at in these terms it makes such thinking look petty and childish, or at least illogical. The only person being damaged in the situation is my friend, and he's doing it to himself.

So, getting back to the seemingly irrational or confounding behaviour of others, let me return to the commuter who insists on sitting in exactly the same seat on her train journey to work every morning.

If she got on the train and asked another passenger to move because they were sitting in 'her seat' then that would be outrageous. In that case her behaviour would be directly affecting an innocent seat occupier, and potentially others in the carriage as they may feel compelled to move as a consequence, if only to distance themselves from such a neurotic nutter. However, remember we're talking about situations that have no impact upon others whatsoever; yet which still seem to possess the power to irritate or annoy some people, and turn others to anger. The woman simply prefers to sit in that seat, and always makes a bee line for it, assuming it's empty. If you're that wrapped up about it why not beat her to it and sit there yourself, just to see how she reacts? Better still, get up earlier, use some unnecessary petrol, drive to an earlier station, occupy 'her seat' and then watch her face when she gets on a few minutes later?

OK, you might think that I'm using exaggeration to prove my point. Sadly, however, it is no exaggeration, as another acquaintance told me that this is exactly what he did one morning!

Victor Meldrew famously got annoyed by the person across the road that left his lights on in his house most of the time. A behaviour that did not directly affect Victor in the slightest, yet which seemed to occupy a significant amount of his time and attention, observing this from his bedroom window and pointing it out to his harangued wife, Margaret.

Maybe such minor behaviours don't even register, let alone irritate you, and you can happily skip forwards – both literally and metaphorically. However, as my Nan used to say… "There's nowt as queer as folk", and some people do let things such as this annoy them.

My challenge to you, the 'normal' reader, is to ask yourself what it is about other people's behaviour that is capable of 'getting your goat', pulling your 'tail feather' or that causes you to get up on your soapbox?

If you identify with any of this, and you want to do something about it then the good news is that this first group of mild irritants are easy to deal with, and we're going to take our first lesson in doing so from a popular female TV comic, Catherine Tate.

## "Am I Bovvered?"

Those who have seen the UK comedy sketch show starring Catherine Tate, in which she plays a range of comic sketch show characters, will know Lauren, the adolescent girl with the *"Am I bothered?"* catch phrase (which she pronounces 'bovvered'), quickly followed by a string of expressions such as:

"Do I look bovvered?"

"Is this face bovvered?"

"Bovvered? Me? Bovvered?"

"I am *NOT* Bovvered!"

... to further accentuate the fact that she is not in the slightest bit bothered, fazed or influenced by what has just happened or been said.

This attitude has pervaded society in other ways, most notably in the use of the term "Whatever!" as a means of indicating that you really couldn't give a shit, or you're dismissive of what another person thinks or is proposing to do.

Of course the joke in the comedy sketch is that Lauren really *is* bothered; a case of 'The lady doth protest too much', though I hesitate to use the term 'lady'; if you've seen the show you will know what I mean.

Within humour lies a grain of truth, and the sketch show illustrates the importance of genuinely not allowing yourself to be affected by a problem or situation. Or, even if you *are* influenced, it demonstrates the power of having the presence of mind, control and composure to not allow yourself to become overly concerned or worried about it.

- He slurps his soup – so what?
- She always has to sit in the same seat in our staff restaurant – so what?
- He makes himself a drink in the staff kitchen, but never asks me if I want one – so what?

If none of these petty annoyances affect you directly then at least take some heart in the fact that you're not shackled by such limiting behaviours. After all, you have options; you have the confidence to be able to choose *any* vacant seat in the staff restaurant, you can make a point by going to get a drink for yourself, *and* for 'Mr.Selfish Ignorant Pig'!

So, when you next find yourself being irritated by people and situations such as these, take a leaf out of Catherine Tate's book:

| | |
|---|---|
| **Tactic:**  | "Am I bothered?" |
| | "Do I look bothered?" |
| | "Bothered...?" |
| | "Face... bothered?" |
| | "Me... bothered?" |
| | "I am *NOT* bloody bothered!" |

The person behaving in this manner is probably not aware of their self-imposed, narrow-minded ritualistic behaviour, or may be deriving some small pleasure or comfort from these activities, in which case let them get on with it.

Sadly, the behaviour may be a symptom of a deeper personality disorder such as Obsessive Compulsive Disorder (OCD) in which an individual becomes trapped in a repetitive meaningless or even detrimental behaviour. However, the boundaries between psychotic, psychiatric and normal psychological behaviours are notoriously blurred.

When does a concern for hygiene and sensible cleanliness flip over to an obsessive compulsion with sterility and repetitive hand washing? At what point does caring for and loving your pet translate into an unwholesome and unnatural obsession with dressing it up in designer dog wear, feeding it from a porcelain plate at the dinner table and letting it sleep in your bed?

*Whatever?*

| | |
|---|---|
| **Tactic:**  | If it doesn't impact upon you in any way, then move on – you've got more important things to focus upon, haven't you? |

## Don't Cut Your Nose Off

Have you ever walked out of a shop, away from a good deal, or away from a product that you had already decided you were going to buy, simply because you didn't like or respect the sales person, and consequently you didn't want them to get credit for the sale? In other words, you consciously and deliberately threw away the logical and tangible benefits of a good deal by allowing emotion to affect your decision. Because you had taken a dislike to another person, your determination that they shouldn't get anything out of the situation over-rode common sense, meaning that you didn't get what you wanted either.

This is what we call a 'lose/lose' situation. They lose and you lose; you both lose; they don't get what they want and neither do you; you create two losers; clever stuff huh!

What is particularly interesting about this situation is that whether the other person gains anything from the deal e.g. a few pounds in sales commission, *does not affect you in any tangible way.* It has no relevant, practical, or substantive effect on your life. If the salesman makes £100 commission for selling you a plasma screen television, and this enables him to take his partner out for a nice meal that evening, does their going out for dinner impact your life in any way whatsoever? Of course not.

Taking another example, what about relationships, particularly when on a 'rebound'? Do you know people who've gone out after being dumped and found someone else, anyone else, no matter how unsuitable, but they do it anyway just to get back at their former partner?

There have been extreme cases of individuals committing suicide, and indeed there was an horrific case reported in the UK press just this week (at time of 1st edition publication in 2008) where a father gassed himself and his two young children in their family car, just to 'get back at his wife'. The suicide note that read 'I've left you a little present, and I am going to make the papers in the morning.'

Sick - as drastic an act as it's possible to imagine.

My thoughts are for the poor innocent kids who probably had no awareness of what was happening... we hope.

My point is that making decisions when you're feeling bad or in an un-resourceful state means that you're likely to make a bad decision because you're not thinking straight, you're not in control; you're acting out of spite, greed, revenge, desperation or some other negative emotional state.

| | |
|---|---|
| **Tactic:**  | Don't make significant decisions when you're feeling bad, angry or in any other unhelpful emotional state.<br><br>Sleep on it; take a fresh view in the morning. You'll probably feel different and make a better choice as a result. |

## Use Other People's Limitations to Your Benefit

Okay, putting bad decisions, relationship breakdowns and vindictive suicides aside, let's lighten things a little.

I'm going to use the very simple and common example of re-fuelling your car at a petrol station to illustrate my next point, and to explain a more general principle. Once you grasp the beautiful simplicity of this concept you will find multiple examples of your own that you can use to make your life easier in many other ways.

This simple technique is based upon uncovering opportunities that arise from other people's ignorance. However, it's critical to stress that this is not about Machiavellian exploitation or malice. The ignorant, let's call them 'less enlightened' people, are in no way compromised or hurt by your actions; in fact they often benefit from them. So think of this as a way for you to make things easier for yourself without cost to anyone else. A 'win' for you, and a 'neutral outcome' for the other person at worse.

Back to the petrol pump...

Have you ever noticed a line of cars forming at a petrol station for a particular pump, even though there are other pumps which dispense exactly the same type and grade of fuel them which are free from customers?

Having observed this behaviour myself on many occasions I've realised that some people seem to feel the need to refuel their car from a pump that is positioned on the same side as their car's petrol cap. Yet, as you may already have found out (or you will when you try it), virtually every petrol pump has a fuel hose long enough to reach around to the other side of a large MPV. Indeed some even have booms that swing out overhead to facilitate re-fuelling from either side of the vehicle.

However, the fact that pump hoses are long enough to reach around to the other side of a car seems to have eluded a significant slice of the public, who wait patiently in line for the pump on the 'correct' side. Of course they're probably not waiting patiently at all. I can almost hear them now as they curse under their breath...

*"For goodness' sake, how long is he going to be? He's already reversed up to the pump twice; can't he see there's a queue?"*

*"Now what's the problem? He's just fiddling with the petrol cap. At this rate we'll be late for dinner. Look, the guy at the pump in front of this idiot is driving away, but the way this chap's parked there's no way I can get around him."*

*"Oh I really don't believe it (Victor?). Look he's trying to put in an exact amount of fuel. He slowed up as he got near to £20:00, and because it tipped over to £20:01 he's now carrying on to £21:00. Aaaarrrrrgggghhhh it's happened again! Now he's got to carry on filling till he gets to exactly £22:00."*

*"If he doesn't hurry up I'm going to ram that super premium hose right up his unleaded arse!"*

Please, allow me some poetic licence, even though it's more worthy of Bernard Manning than William Wordsworth. This is the stuff of heart attacks, or at the very least, unnecessary stress; which may of course ultimately contribute to a premature death. However, you don't need to die before your time, you can make a far more enlightened response to such situations.

Rather than be the person in the queue who's ranting about the guy at the pump, why not decide instead to capitalise upon this simple and common situation for your own benefit and continued sanity? Let others sit in the 'collective ignorance queue', whilst you drive up smartly to the first available pump, regardless of whether it's to your right or left; fill, pay and go? You're not hurting anyone, and in fact you're contributing to the efficiency of the process for all concerned because it's one less car adding to the queue for a particular pump. For extra enjoyment, you could always glance into your rear-view mirror as you drive away, to catch the looks of exasperation and frustration from those still queuing at the station behind you, who's annoyance may now be compounded by the fact that you managed to fill up and pay quicker than them.

I use this deliberately facile example, not to show you how to make the chore of fuelling your car as quick as possible, but rather to illustrate a more general principle; that alternative courses of action often reveal themselves when you examine the 'normal', less productive behaviours of other people.

Furthermore, far from being a selfish act, your technique at the petrol station is actually helpful, as in the process you're revealing a time-saving tip to others. They've got little else to do whilst they queue on the other side, so why not help them out with an altruistic performance which demonstrates an alternative response to an everyday situation? Unfortunately, your philanthropic gesture will result in diminishing returns for yourself, as the more people who cotton on to your cunning technique, the fewer vacant pumps you will find in the future. But then you'll be thinking a couple of steps ahead, won't you.

Here's another simple driving-related example to which most readers will be able to relate.

You're approaching a roundabout on a dual carriageway and you need to turn left to get into town. Unfortunately almost everyone else wants to do the same thing, so there's a large queue on the left whilst the right hand lane which heads out into the countryside is relatively free. One solution is to move into the right hand lane, approach the roundabout indicating right, continue all the way around the roundabout as you're legally entitled to do, and then, as you approach your exit, indicate left and turn off to town.

Again, I give this simple example, not because the tip is useful in and of itself, but rather to make the wider point of encouraging you to think more broadly around life's everyday inconveniences and frustrations, and to consider smarter ways of responding. Don't sit in your car 'smarting... decide instead to get 'smart'.

Whilst on most occasions your actions don't negatively impact other people, such as in the petrol pump scenario, this example does show that there are other situations in which your behaviour is a little sneakier. By entering the roundabout ahead of those who have patiently queued to turn left, you momentarily hold up the left hand queue when you exit a few seconds later. However, I should imagine that even the most neurotic driver will still be able to sleep at night after (literally) pulling off this manoeuvre. If you can't then I suggest that for peace of mind at least, you go back to sitting patiently in life's left hand lane.

Before we drive on, you might like to spend some time dreaming up your own creative solutions to everyday situations such as these, and email me with your ideas. Remember, the general tactic I recommend is:

| | |
|---|---|
| **Tactic:**<br> | Capitalise upon situations where others unnecessarily constrain themselves, provided you don't harm them in the process.<br><br>Combine this with the earlier tactic of maintaining, creating or actively looking for a range of options, and you will rarely find yourself stuck without an alternative course of action. |

## "Just Thinking of Him Makes My Flesh Creep"

Do you ever find yourself becoming irritated by people, even when they are not in the same room, building, town, country or continent as yourself?

When you think of a person that you don't like;

· What do you think about?

· What sequence of images do you project onto the video-screen of your mind?

· What sounds do you surround yourself with; what do you hear them saying and how are they saying it?

· What do you tell yourself?

· What feelings are associated with all of the above?

· What emotions do you begin to experience?

If you're normal then these will be largely negative in nature, probably involving a re-run of a well worn mental video that you've created. Typically this will revolve around a painful, awkward, embarrassing, difficult or otherwise frustrating situation, not only re-enacted, but also expertly directed by you. It will be in full glorious 3-D Technicolor with Dolby™ surround sound, the only things missing being the big heads obscuring your view, the popcorn sellers, mobile phones going off and a suspiciously sticky carpet.

Note, above all else, how this short self-generated 'video sequence' is capable of making you feel bad _instantaneously_. Also, notice that _you_ did it to _yourself_.

What's happening is you're allowing unpleasant memories of encounters with another person, or self-constructed imaginary future scenarios with this individual or group, to act as a negative trigger in your mind. This trigger, when 'fired off', automatically makes you feel bad. Imagine a button being pushed in the sequence:

PRESS → CLICK → WHIRR → BAD FEELING

An predictable chain reaction of pre-programmed sequences that happens automatically and instantly.

What's even worse is that the other person is not consciously trying to make you feel bad right now; they're not even in the room. You're doing it for them; you're pushing the button for them, repeatedly. They could be sunning themselves on a beach in Malibu, steaming in the hot springs of Iceland's Blue Lagoon, or enjoying a meal with friends at home. Meanwhile, you're stewing in a home-made soup of inner turmoil, inadequacy, hatred, self-loathing or deep-seated resentment. Okay, perhaps I'm exaggerating to make my point, but not even Iceland's Blue Lagoon can claim to be that hot and caustic, and as far as cooking the soup goes, you've refined the recipe to perfection over the years.

So, if you find yourself feeling bad just by thinking about a particular person, then you're allowing them to annoy you in your spare time. If the scenario is a work context and you're using your precious weekend to do this thinking then that's doubly galling. What's worse, they don't need to invest any of their own time as you're doing the work for both of you by repeating and amplifying their annoyance, over and over in your mind. How crazy is that?

So, it's possible for a person to allow themselves to be irritated by someone, even when they're not in their presence. It's possible, *but it doesn't have to be that way*. In Chapter Two we discussed the importance of being fully in charge of your own mind; after all, if you're not in charge of you, then who is? So we're agreed that you're not going to allow people to mentally mess with you, and the key question therefore is how and why do we do this?

The bad news is that in the past, most people have taught themselves to react in a negative unhelpful way to these triggers, probably over many years. The good news is that you can re-program yourself to react positively, and you can do this much faster than the bad programming took to install. We're talking seconds and minutes, not months or years.

Try some of the techniques below and find out what works best for you.

## Install a Personal 'Cinema Surround System' – *For Free!*

Instead of the normal way in which you think about and represent this person in your mind, which may be as intimidating, aggressive, annoying, sarcastic, bullying etcetera, try this instead.

Make a picture of them in your mind which is the opposite of how you normally view them. You might imagine them as a rather pathetic individual in a weak or feeble situation, possibly whimpering or defensive.

Now before you get too far into this, you need to make some changes relating to the *way* in which you are seeing this in your mind's eye.

It's likely that up until now you have been imagining a previously negative situation in full Technicolor with accompanying cinema surround sound. Imagining negative images in this way is not going to help you because it's a bit like projecting the image onto a massive cinema screen which consumes your attention and leaves no room for anything of a more helpful nature. So, instead of taking your mind off to the metaphorical multiplex, imagine you're now viewing the person or situation on a small, fuzzy, black and white television on the other side of the room. The scene is still visible to you in your mind's eye, but way off in the distance. Try it now, and see how small, distant, fuzzy, distorted and colourless you can make the image, and how tinny, crackly and pathetic you can make the sound track.

Did you do it? Could you see and hear it?

Don't read on until you have done this.

As you imagine the scene now, are you starting to feel different about this person already? If not, you need to do it again, and to try harder this time, as the process should only take a few seconds if you're doing it right.

Practice with this for a while, experimenting by switching between the full-colour, full-on surround sound, and possibly intimidating 'in-your-face' images, and then the small, black and white, crackly, tinny, distant pathetic images. You should find that your negative emotions diminish when you think about the situation in the second manner, and they return when you think about it in wide-screen, full on, full colour format.

Assuming this mental exercise is having a real impact upon you, your goal now is to eliminate the previous full-on images, and to have fully replaced them in your mind, with the pathetic, distant and blurred images. You're turning this person's previously perceived 'importance' into 'impotence'. Any time you catch yourself imagining the situation in the previous manner you must immediately switch to the blurred, distant, black and white image with poor audio quality.

---

**Tactic:**

Change how you represent the person or the situation within your mind by using the video and sound replacement technique above.

Remember, you are the 'cinema projector operator' of your own mind; you decide what's 'Now Showing'.

---

Now the fun bit. Picture yourself as all powerful, confident, courageous, strong and assertive. If you want to go to extremes, imagine yourself as a giant or some other form of strong, dominating beast about to bear down upon them from above.

Don't laugh. If you think this is a load of old b******s then it won't work for you – *guaranteed!* Equally, if you open your mind for a moment and give it a go, then you should start to notice some changes in the way you think and feel about people and situations, and all this within just a few minutes.

Imagine yourself saying, or better still if you cannot be overheard, shout aloud in a voluminous and commanding voice something along the lines of… "Now I've got you, you can't hurt me you pathetic excuse for a life form, born out of unlawful procreation… *your ass is mine!*"

It helps tremendously if you stomp around as you vocalise this; just make sure that nobody's in and the windows are closed; or, if you're in a hotel room, expect a knock at the door within 10 minutes!

You can have some fun with this, such as imagining them naked and cowering behind their desk, because the more you exaggerate the more your emotional state will change. The more you alter your internal representation of this person the more powerful and impactful the technique will become.

When you run this imaginary sequence several times, and repeat it over the next few days, you will find that you are less intimidated when you meet this person in real life. They may even start to appear as weak, ineffectual and pathetic, or reveal themselves as the frightened cowards that they really are.

The reality won't change dramatically overnight, but your confidence in dealing with this person, and how you view them will, which will affect the dynamics of your future interactions. From that point forward they will have progressively less negative impact upon you, and like a warlock or wizard losing their powers, they will become impotent.

Now here's some double magic...

---

**Tactic:**

When you want to enhance or emphasise *positive* experiences then use the full-on, up close, glorious Technicolour surround sound method.

When it's a 'movie' you want to see and remember, you wouldn't watch it on a crummy little 'black and shite' television. By taking a moment to think about your thinking, you can conjure up inspirational and empowering blockbusters in an instant... and for free.

---

## Change the Recording

> *"Wagner's music is better than it sounds."*
>
> Mark Twain

Have you ever had the experience of finding yourself caught up and trapped in an 'audio loop'; a psychological state where you find yourself 'speaking' unhelpful, negative internal dialogue and thoughts over and over again? Many of us do this, and we're not even aware at a conscious level how much time we spend occupying our thinking and internal dialogue with this literal litter.

It doesn't have to be negative of course; it could simply be a meaningless phrase, or a couple of lines from a song that you can't seem to get out of your head. However, if the dialogue is unhelpful and negative, then you need to pay special attention, as you've caught yourself up in a progressively damaging, vicious internal dialogue cycle.

For example, imagine you're going through a challenging time at work with your boss or a colleague, you're in a difficult relationship with someone or you're worried about the health of a close family member. It's common to find yourself spending a large proportion of your waking hours allowing these thoughts to consume you, yet they're not helping you in any way. You have trapped yourself within a 'negative thought loop' like a vinyl record that's stuck in a single circular groove; and the longer you plough the groove, the deeper those thoughts become ingrained.

What do you do when an old-fashioned vinyl record becomes stuck in this way and you find yourself listening to a constantly repeated phrase? You give the record a jolt, you re-position the needle or you change the record. Simple. So, in exactly the same way, when you find yourself trapped in repeated negative and unhelpful internal dialogue, you need to take action to jolt yourself out of it, change it or throw it away for good.

However, simply turning off the record or throwing it away is only half the solution; it will have a nasty habit of coming back. After all, you've trained yourself to think about it in this way for some time now, so like a song that's stuck in your mind, it's difficult to keep it out of your head.

Have you ever tried to think of nothing? It's difficult, because your mind needs to keep active, it needs to be constantly stimulated, even when you're asleep, which is one of the reasons you dream. So, part two of the solution is to replace the record with a brand new one; one that is more helpful to your purpose. Maybe this time it's not a record, but an MP3 track that you can 'skip and jump'. Even that sounds better than being 'stuck in a groove'.

Whilst it's difficult not to think of anything, we also know that it's not possible to think about more than one thing at the same time. Sure, we can think of several things within a short period of time, but they are sequential not concurrent. Can you read two different books simultaneously for example? No. If you were stupid enough to want to do this then what you would actually find yourself doing is reading a few words of each, switching every second or so between pages, and confusing yourself in the process. That said, it might make for an extremely interesting story, with abrupt and unusual twists and turns in plot line.

Similarly, imagine trying to do mental arithmetic whilst also having a conversation with someone, it just doesn't work. How you feel when you're trying to talk to someone who says they're listening, whilst at the same time they continue to read a newspaper?

So the solution to all of these situations is to work *with* your brain, and to capitalise on the fact that it's not possible for you to think of two things at the same time. The solution is to consciously occupy your mind with *alternative* thoughts of a positive and helpful nature. When you install these words and images successfully it will be impossible for you to simultaneously think about the previously unhelpful thoughts. The trick is to keep the positive stuff there for as long as possible so there's little opportunity for the 'nasties' to creep back in.

At a practical level there are at least four things that you can do:

**Tactic:** Consciously think about something else – this can be effective, but tends to work only for short periods, as the other thoughts come back to haunt you when you stop doing this consciously.

**Tactic:** Play music, especially positive, uplifting inspirational music. Again this can help, but it's still possible to be thinking about negative things whilst listening to music, at a sub-conscious level i.e. you catch yourself drifting into those thoughts again. Singing along to the music helps further, but again, some techniques are best practiced alone.

**Tactic:** Read something – now this is more powerful because to read you need to engage your conscious brain. However, as any reader will know, it's possible to find yourself mechanically reading the words on the page without fully registering them or taking in their meaning; meanwhile those nasty thoughts have crept in again.

**Tactic:** Get involved in an all-consuming activity, preferably something mentally and/or physically complex.

This last technique is one of the best for banishing unwanted thoughts from your mind because you're fully engaging most of your senses simultaneously. It's impossible to fully and actively contribute to a complex mental or physical activity, especially if it involves other people, whilst thinking about something else, at least not in any depth or for any significant length of time.

The exceptions would be repetitive solo physical exercise such as running, or rowing, where there is little to occupy your mind, and so activities such as this invite the mind to wander because the brain needs and wants to be stimulated. It's at times like this when the negative internal dialogue 'thought loops' are most likely to creep back in. Team sports are ideal in combating this mental dis-ease, as in addition to taking your mind off negative thoughts, you get a great endorphin-boosting exercise in the process.

Admittedly, when the activity finishes you risk reverting to negative thoughts again, but at least you've given yourself a significant break. Maybe part of the solution is to increase the number and range of activities that you do so that there's even less opportunity for the nasties to nip in unnoticed.

For the less physically able or active there are plenty of compelling films that you can engage with or novels in which to lose yourself… to mentally lose yourself.

Okay, having spent the first part of this book getting our own thinking in order, we are now going to move on to uncover a whole raft of tactics that we can use to deal with the things that other people say and do.

# Chapter 7

## Cunning Linguistics

# 7
# Cunning Linguistics

**Overheard on a Plane, Train or Automobile ...**

**... on Tennis Courts and in Law Courts**

*"I know you don't like me."*

*"That's pathetic."*

*"I'm late because of you."*

*"Everyone knows he's a failure."*

*"You shouldn't do that."*

*"He's much better respected."*

*"My husband's such an idiot."*

*"Her behaviour is totally unacceptable."*

*"You just can't trust some people."*

*"He's absolutely brilliant."*

*"You make me mad."*

*"I know she doesn't care."*

*"That's not a good look."*

*"It's better not to have children."*

*"You bloody two-faced liar!"*

Shall I go on?

No, it's too depressing.

But in all seriousness, how would you deal with these statements if they were spoken to you or about you? After all, many of them are the sort of things that you hear every day.

Would you just blubber and bluster, agree or disagree, avoid or avert, or attack like a whirling dervish with a dose of Victor's vitreol? As discussed in Chapter Two, you have a choice in how you respond.

And what if you heard such things being said of other people? If you wanted to step in to challenge such assertions, would you know how to do so in a way that is likely to yield positive results, as opposed to exacerbating the situation or receiving a bloody nose?

## A Toolkit for Verbally 'Pushing Back'

For many readers, this section will contain the most compelling, insightful and useful ideas for how to deal effectively with how other people behave, and particularly with what they say. After all, short of avoidance or running away at one end of the scale, and hand-to-hand combat or physical attack and torture at the other, for most day-to-day interactions the quality of your outcome will be dependent upon how you choose to respond verbally, in the moment.

Please remember that this book is not intended to teach you how to win friends and influence people by being a 'nice person'. It certainly has a strong focus upon effective communications, but that doesn't always mean 'nice' communications. My primary purpose is to help you to deal with people who do not have your best interests at heart, and who are trying to manipulate you, other people or the situation to their own ends. In short, I will show you how to fight fire with a range of verbal fire-extinguishers, but also with fire itself.

With that in mind, the techniques that I present here are unashamedly challenging, provocative and in some cases confrontational. This is because some people just don't, can't or won't play fair. They will try to manipulate you with both *what* they say and the *way* in which they say it.

Some are very clever and cunning about this; they are the social and political foxes of society and organisations. Other, less-sophisticated individuals just try their best to twist things in a way that suits their means. They can be blunt, awkward and unsophisticated in their approach. They too are motivated towards their own ends, but rather than use the surgical precision of a surgeon's scalpel they resort to the ham-fisted impact of a club hammer.

Then there's a whole bunch of 'innocents' who don't even realise the degree to which they're distorting reality; the 'innocent lambs' or 'inept donkeys' of the corporate and social world.

Faced with such verbal provocation from others, and an unfair starting point that's not of your making, it's only right that you equip yourself with as many linguistic tools as possible to deal effectively with these situations. You need to be tooled up to turn the tables on, and undermine the unsubstantiated arguments, statements and assertions of such people.

In order to achieve this I will show you how others have learned to mislead, manipulate and distort the truth. I am NOT advocating that you use their tactics. However, in order to defend yourself from underhand verbal manoeuvres, you must at least be aware of the 'slings and arrows' that can be used against you.

I will show you how to use language to clarify language, and in this way you will be able to anticipate, dodge, parry, defend, push back, and where appropriate, fight back.

Therefore, this chapter will focus upon how you can respectfully challenge what other people say. It will help you to win arguments, get to the truth in situations, and stop people in their tracks when they try to get away with distorting reality or unfairly manipulating the situation.

## Learning from Examples

The way I can best illustrate these techniques, without getting us caught up in too many 'nominalisations', 'complex-equivalences', 'lost performatives' or other linguistically confusing terms, is through a series of everyday examples; the sort of things that you hear people saying in day-to-day conversation.

As an aside, I find it interesting that linguists and lexicographers, in their attempts to explain and catalogue our language tend to avoid common, everyday terms, which is paradoxical when you think about it. The academic stance often seems to be... "Why say spade when you can say digging implement?" Some academics are more likely to get excited upon discovering a 'lack of referential index' or an inappropriately inserted 'universal quantifier' than at the prospects of a great night out with their mates – if they have any!

So, following the everyday examples I've then suggested a range of possible responses. Each scenario, whilst interesting in its own right, illustrates a general principle that you can then apply in future situations, regardless of the content or context.

You will immediately see from these examples how the particular response you choose can dramatically change the dynamics and direction of the conversation; sometimes turning it 180 degrees. Often you will succeed in putting the other person on the 'back foot', leaving you firmly in control.

In the process of working through the examples you will be educating and fine-tuning your mind, and raising your conscious awareness of some of the linguistic tricks and games that people play. Your goal should be to move from a position where you currently have to consciously spot these tricks and deal with them in the moment, to one in which you do this elegantly, unconsciously and almost magically!

##  Health Warning

There are occasions where, in order to illustrate a point, we need to go to a level of detail that some may consider is bordering on anality. However, we're often told...

> *"The devil is in the detail."*

I'm going to teach you to be a cunning linguist, a conjuror of potent verbal spells, the casting of which will leave your audience 'wand-ering' just how you managed to so effortlessly disarm them.

In linguistics, the 'tricks' often lie buried in the detail of what people say and in how they say it; i.e. the emphasis or intonation.

To make my point, examine the very last sentence that you just read. Does this mean that the tricks lie buried, as in 'deep down', or could it mean that they 'lie', as in 'untruthful', and at the same time these are all the more insidious because they're under the surface, buried deep?

Remember, the power of language is mostly hidden at the 'unconscious' level, and so in this chapter we will be drilling into and exposing this to discover 'where the truth lies'. We are also told that 'knowledge is power', and so a deeper knowledge of how language can be used and abused will ensure that you stay one step ahead in the language and influence game.

In the examples that follow I've called the person who is being irrational, irritating, challenging, aggressive, manipulative or otherwise awkward, the 'Provocateur'. I've also structured the chapter into a series of eight 'crimes' that these people commonly commit, the first of which is to use 'subjective slurs and meaningless labels'.

Your role is two-fold; you are both a detective and a respondent. Let the crime scene unfold...

## Crime #1: Using Subjective Slurs and Meaningless Labels

Words themselves do not 'mean' anything. People use words to express what they mean. In the process of expressing what they mean, people can, also be mean.

With our forensic gloves on, here's our first case:

Provocateur:              *"He's such a jerk."*

Response 1:               "He's been *acting* like a jerk, has he?"

Before you read on, consider this very short interaction. In particular, what do you notice about the response?

Try to come up with at least two separate observations that are significant in terms of what you think the response is trying to achieve. Resist any temptation to read on until you've come up with at least two relevant points.

**Analysis:**

This reply to the provocateur does at least three things, and all of this in just eight words:

- It puts the behaviour into the past (*'He's been acting'*), opening up the possibility that the person in question has now stopped doing this.

- It directs attention to the behaviour (*'acting like'*), and so away from the personal insult (*'a jerk'*). Someone may 'act' the fool; it doesn't necessarily mean that they *are* a fool or deserve to be branded as such for life.

- It questions the evidence and/or the opinion of the person by turning the response into a question (*"He's been acting like a jerk, has he?"*)

Did you pick up on any of these points?

Now here's the same provocation, but with a different response:

Provocateur:          *"He's such a jerk."*

Response 2:          *"So he's been acting in a way that you don't like, has he?"*

What's different about this reply?

Once again, before you read on have a go at deconstructing this, much as a detective would meticulously pick apart the details of a scene of crime, to see what you can learn from this alternative response.

## Analysis:

This reply is stronger than the first, and there are at least three new observations that we can make:

- It completely removes the derogatory insult (no reference this time in the response to the word "jerk"). This weakens and dilutes the provocateur's statement through the technique of 're-phrasing', a technique to which we will often return.

- It unexpectedly shifts the pressure on to the speaker as it implies that it is *they* who may be the one with the problem ('...*acting in a way that you don't like'*).

- The response removes any value judgement from the behaviour, i.e. 'behaving' in a way that you don't like does not mean that the behaviour is either a 'good' or a 'bad' thing; it neutralises it.

Let's now lift ourselves out of the detail of this first example and summarise what we can learn from just two one-line responses to a single provocative statement.

Firstly, by not openly agreeing with the provocateur you actually do more than simply remain neutral; the unstated implication is that you disagree. Notice that this was achieved in both instances by responding with a question rather than a statement. This is an important point to which we will return later in this chapter.

'Jerk', 'moron', 'idiot', 'waster'... these are all examples of derogatory terms that are often bandied around in conversation, regardless of social circle. I once attended a very classy dinner party that deteriorated into a heightened emotional slanging match, culminating in the slamming of doors, a screeching of tyres on gravel and several plates of untouched gourmet food. I hasten to add that I was an interested observer of this scene rather than an instigator, promoter or target.

However, labels such as these are meaningless without concrete substance. If someone called you a thief or an alcoholic then you would be left in no doubt as to what they were accusing you of. However, what exactly is a 'jerk' or a 'waster'?

In the UK at present, it's common for kids to insult each other by calling them 'gay', even though in some cases the younger ones don't even know the meaning of the word. My own son hurled this label at me recently when he stormed out of the room after an argument, accompanied by the ritualistic and seemingly compulsory door-slamming.

Now, is he suggesting that I engage in sexual encounters with men? I don't think so.

In a letter to 'The Times' this week, a reader recalled an incident when he asked a young person to stop riding his bicycle on the pavement. This innocuous and perfectly reasonable request resulted in the kid accusing him of being a 'poof, pervert and paedophile'. It's amazing how such specific and immediately insightful deductions can be made by a child about a complete stranger, solely on the basis of a three-second interaction; if only it were that easy to identify paedophiles in our society.

Having said that, maybe it's not so surprising. A few years ago a mob-rule mentality developed in some parts of the UK when several paediatricians were targeted by well-intentioned, though clearly illiterate, vigilantes.

Back in more normal circumstances, whenever you hear inappropriate labels being applied you can choose to challenge them by asking *what specifically* it is that the person is doing that deserves such a derogatory label.

More often than not, people will generalise, compartmentalise and slur others on the flimsiest of evidence, or no evidence whatsoever, particularly if they've decided they don't like them.

| | |
|---|---|
| **Counter tactics:**  | Challenge inappropriate and meaningless labels. |
| | Dilute the venom of provocations by subtly changing the words that are used by others. |
| | Respond with a question that questions and challenges some aspect of the assertion. |

We can apply this principle of challenging labels to any intangible descriptor, for example:

Provocateur:     *"That's rubbish!"*

Response 1:      "What do you mean by "rubbish"; can you be more specific?"

Response 2:      "What exactly is "rubbish" about it?"

What observations can you make about these responses? Give this some thought before reading on. You'll learn far more from this chapter if you do your own thinking and analysis first, and then check this against the points noted below.

## Analysis:

These replies:

- Show that you're not prepared to accept broad brush value judgements at face value.
- Challenge the speaker to substantiate their opinion with tangible facts and evidence.
- Force them to be specific about what they *mean* by 'rubbish', which might then enable you to challenge their subjective judgement in a more objective manner.

It's the same as someone saying that something is 'nice'. Well, it's nice that it's nice, but what does nice mean and what is it in particular that makes it 'nice'?

Of course there's every chance that in reply to your challenge about what exactly constitutes 'rubbish' you'll get a clear account of exactly what *is* wrong with the item in question and why. In which case, you've achieved your objective; you've clarified the facts and established something tangible. If you then want to dispute the facts you could go on to present counter-evidence.

The point is that you're now able to deal with tangible evidence that is grounded in reality, rather than unsubstantiated opinions wrapped up in meaningless labels.

| **Counter tactics:**  | *"When you say 'X', what do you mean by 'X'?"* |
| --- | --- |
| | *"In what way specifically…?"* |
| | *"How specifically…?"* |

Here's another way of responding to the same claim, by taking a complete 180 degree turn:

Provocateur:     *"That's rubbish!"*

Response 3:     "What's *not* rubbish about it?"

How would you react if you were the provocateur and received this response? It might throw you off balance a little, right? So why is that? What gives this response its particular power?

**Analysis:**

This reply:

- Doesn't argue that there are things that might be 'rubbish'. Remember that by not agreeing with a statement you signal neutrality as a minimum, and disagreement by implication.

- Dramatically re-directs attention to those aspects that are 'good', or at least not so 'bad'. If asked to describe what's 'good' about something, you have to stop, even if only momentarily, thinking about what's bad about it. If someone asks you what you liked about a film you'd just seen, or a meal that you had eaten, you *have* to think about the good things in order to answer the question. This is the case even if you do not want to openly admit to there being anything good about it. Remember we discussed in Chapter 6 how it is impossible to think of two different things simultaneously.

- Challenges the provocateur to be balanced and reasonable in their assessment. If they cannot find anything good in something, when clearly there are redeeming features, then it exposes their bias and calls their judgement in other areas into question.

**Counter tactics:**     *"What's* not *'X' about it?"*

*"In what ways could the opposite be true?"*

Remember that people will also attach meaningless labels that are positive, such as 'brilliant', 'excellent', 'fabulous', 'top quality' and of course, the ubiquitous 'nice'. The good news is that in the interests of promoting clear communication and understanding you can use exactly the same technique in these situations. All you have to do is ask what exactly it is that's 'brilliant' or 'excellent' about it?

For example, imagine you've just delivered a presentation at work and a colleague comes up to you to say they think you did a 'brilliant job'. What you really need to know is what *specifically* it was that you did to make this positive impression. 'Brilliant job' is great to hear, but it doesn't help you in any tangible way; you don't know what it is that you need to continue to do in order to repeat this success in the future.

An example of the last point might be that you give someone close to you open honest feedback about some of the ways in which they are letting themselves down, e.g. in terms of behaviour or dress sense. It's precisely because you do care and respect the person that you take the trouble to tell them. Someone who did not respect the individual, or a person who was afflicted with CBA Syndrome (Can't Be Arsed) may just simply walk away and say nothing.

So you can see that with this small collection of counter tactics alone, found at just one 'crime scene', you are able to cut through a whole swathe of misinformation, bias and prejudice in one sweep.

With this in mind, here are a couple of extended examples of how you might respond to someone who puts either a positive or negative frame around a subject. You may notice that in my enthusiasm I've slipped in some new angles of questioning, but don't worry as we'll return to these later in this chapter:

Provocateur:     *"He's the best student in the class."*

Responses:       "What do you mean by 'best'?"

"What is it specifically that sets him apart in your eyes?"

"In which areas would you not consider him to be the best?"

"Who might not consider him to be the best?"

Provocateur:     *"You don't respect me."*

Responses:       "What does 'respect' mean to you?"

"What is it that I'm doing, or not doing that makes you think I don't respect you?"

"How would you know that I respected you?"

"In what ways could some of the things I do that you don't like me doing, actually mean that I *do* respect you?"

You'll remember from Chapter Five how we explored the benefits and insights that come from 'reverse thinking', which is the basis of the last comment.

Our second 'crime' is a 'time crime'.

## Crime #2: Using the Past to Justify the Present

In the unfair world of prejudice, some people continually refer back to, and recount events from some time ago, using this as evidence to substantiate their *current* opinion about a person or situation.

This could of course be either a positive or a negative opinion.

For example, someone says "I'll never forget the time they embarrassed me in front of the team."

On questioning, you discover that this incident occurred seven years ago, yet the speaker is still using it as evidence against the person. The fact that they've not caused embarrassment since appears to be disregarded, such is the emotion attached to a seven-year personal grudge.

Similarly, a person may say "Dave's fantastic, he's just so reliable; do you remember the time he promised to get us tickets for the England 'v' Germany match and we knew he didn't stand a chance, yet he still managed to get the tickets?" This sounds like Dave is indeed a most reliable and trustworthy person, in fact a 'superstar', until you discover that the match in question occurred in 1966! Don't you think there's a chance that 'Dependable Dave' has let someone down in other circumstances during the past 40+ years?

In psychological circles there's a well known phenomenon called 'Halo and Horns'. Put simply, it means that once first impressions are formed, and this can happen remarkably quickly, they can be difficult if not impossible to change.

For example, at a job interview the interviewing manager takes an instant dislike to a candidate. Throughout the remainder of the interview the manager will be unconsciously selective in what they 'hear' the candidate say.

Any answers that confirm the manager's initial bad impression are taken as evidence that the candidate is indeed unsuitable, whilst counter-evidence is filtered out and dismissed. The interviewer has, in effect, already made up their mind, and so their brain is automatically programmed to look for *logical evidence* to substantiate and back up the *emotional decision,* made within a few seconds or minutes, and some time earlier.

In your own social circle or work team, if you decide that you like a person then you tend to only see the 'good' in them, whilst any evidence to the contrary is either dismissed or excused as allowable. However, if the same behaviour were to be exhibited by a person you didn't like, then there's every chance it would be taken as yet more evidence of their failings. Be honest, we're all prone to this form of bias and prejudice. It's another example of those 'normal' things that humans do; but... we don't want to be just 'normal' do we?

So, in terms of counter tactics, by asking for current or at least recent evidence, you're clarifying whether this is still the case or whether we're 'talking history'? If the provocateur admits that the evidence was some time in the past, then the validity of their statement is questioned, and they've only made themselves look foolish. Time moves on, people change, external reality shifts, but attitudes harden, and myths, misrepresentations and misperceptions can remain.

Here's an extended example to illustrate how you might counter this crime in real time; a case of catching the criminal in the act:

Provocateur:     *"He's not to be trusted."*

Response:        "Why do you say that?"

Provocateur:     *"Well, he's been caught stealing."*

Response:        "Really, when was that?"

| | |
|---|---|
| Provocateur: | *"Well, it was some time ago now, before you joined us."* |
| Response: | "Hang on a minute, I've been here for nearly three years now, so has he been stealing things recently?" |
| Provocateur: | *"Well, not that I've heard, but you never know, do you?"* |
| Response: | "And what was it that he stole, exactly?" |
| Provocateur: | *"Oh, just the usual things, you know, stationery and stuff."* |
| Response: | "Stationery huh! Well I guess in that case half the company would be locked up." |
| Provocateur: | *"Right! Who hasn't taken a few pens home before now?"* |

You can see the direction in which this line of enquiry is going, and how the provocateur's initial stark accusation is melting away.

---

**Counter tactics:**

*"Why do you say that?"*

*"When was the last time that ...?"*

*"How often does this happen?"*

*"How many years would have to pass before you would consider it inappropriate for people to drag things up from your own past and to announce them to others?"*

*"Sorry, was that before or after decimalisation?"*

[Tactic: Use of humour]

---

So, they've done the time and paid for their crime. We've managed to redress the imbalance in terms of what's old news and current reality, but what about the criminal who is 'larger than life'? After all, we don't want to allow others to make a drama out of a crisis.

## Crime #3: Using Exaggerated or Value-Laden Descriptions

We've already discussed the tendency people have to use labels, but what makes it worse is when the labels they choose are dramatic, inflammatory or in some way sensationally out of kilter with reality.

I recall an incident in a pizza restaurant when an American lady pushed her chair back noisily, stood up and called in a loud voice to the waitress across the room of diners... "Excuse me Maam, but this pizza's *rancid*!"

Now maybe it wasn't exactly to her taste, but when I think about 'rancid' I imagine a 12" thick crust with toppings of putrefying flesh, green cheese bubbling with sulphurous gases and a meaty sprinkling of big, fat, juicy macrophaging maggots!

Even respected institutions resort to such reality-twisting statements. Just now on the BBC lunchtime news I heard the headline:

> *"Bread and milk prices set to soar, as UK farmland is flooded!"*
>
> BBC Radio 4 – September 2007

When the newsreader elaborated, it transpired that the prediction was for a 10% increase in the price of a loaf of bread and pint of milk over the next nine months. Now is that the sort of price increase you might have imagined for a commodity whose price you've just been told is about to soar? When you calculate that this translates into just a few pennies, you realise that rampant mass hysteria and panic buying is probably not a sensible reaction on this occasion.

By toning down the hyperbole, challenging whether what has just been said is *really* the case, and questioning the degree to which things might have been exaggerated, it's usually possible to bring the conversation down to a more rational level. However, that's just one technique, and a pretty obvious one. An alternative, and often more effective approach, is to take the exaggerated label at face value – *literally,* and to throw it back at the provocateur.

For example:

Provocateur:     *"He's a bad man."*

Response 1:      "Really, you mean like Hitler, Harold Shipman or Saddam Hussein?"

or

Provocateur:     *"He'd eat his own grandmother."*

Response 2:      "What? You mean like Hannibal Lector? Ugh, that's gross!"

If a colleague tells you that they've just been… "Pasted against the walls in a meeting with the CEO'" then you might come back with…

Response:        "What? He *hit* you?"

Now it's important to realise that by reacting in this way you're really just having a bit of fun; 'pulling their leg' so to speak. It's best done with further exaggeration yourself, and a hint of a smile to signal that you know they're distorting the situation grossly, and you're just playing along with their little game. Clearly, you're not so stupid as to think that the speaker really imagines your colleague to be a mass-murdering mother-muncher or that there's literally been a blood bath in the boardroom. What you're doing is deliberately taking their description at face value in order to show how ridiculous it is. By simply responding to their exaggeration, after all *they* said it not you, you're respectfully challenging them to be more realistic, and you're doing it with humour and with a knowing smile.

Have some fun with this; I'm sure you will find plenty of opportunities to practise.

---

**Counter tactics:**

Question whether what has just been said really is the case.

Get people to quantify their statements, e.g. 'When you say "massive" how big was it exactly? Could I fit it into this box?'

Use their exaggeration and turn it back on them in

the form of a clarifying, yet provocative question, as in:

*"A 'Dictator'? What...you mean like Stalin?"*

---

 **Exercise:**

Have a go at dealing with some of these hyperbolic words and expressions in order to get your mind accustomed to challenging and toning down some of the dramatic and wildly-inflated imagery that some people are prone to use:

- *"We were tearing at each other's throats like two dogs in a sack."*

- *"The artwork made me puke."*

- *"Millions face misery as the Bank of England raises base rates by 0.25%"*

- *"He's a dirty little maggot."*

One of my favourites is from a sketch many years ago from the comedian Rowan Atkinson...

- "It's like a blind man in a dark room in the middle of the night, looking for a black cat ... that isn't there."

##  Health Warning

Language is poetry. It can be vivid, highly evocative and endlessly fascinating and enthralling in its descriptions. In no manner am I suggesting that this rich colour palette be diluted, washed over or suppressed. Except, that is, when people abuse the power and beauty of the language that we've been blessed with, in order to distort and twist truth and reality to their own ends.

So, in this section we've made reference to several serial killers and we've learned how to tackle the 'serial-exaggerist', (I just made up that word, by the way), but are you able to resist becoming a 'partner in crime'? Can you push back when others want to co-opt you into their fiendish plans or lure you into their inequitable den of iniquity? Let's examine crime number 4.

### Crime #4: Expecting You to Agree

To illustrate this particular crime I'm returning to our first example: "He's such a jerk."

You will recall from the first two replies that at no time did the respondent openly agree with the provocateur. This was deliberate, as it adds even more power to the response. Let me explain...

Most people, when faced with the assertion "He's such a jerk" will reply with
- "Oh I know."
- "Really, what's he gone and done now?" or
- "Yes, he's such an idiot isn't he?"

However, we've already learned that by not openly agreeing, this in itself is a way of indirectly disagreeing. It's not only what you *say* that influences another person, it's also what you noticeably *do not say*.

For example, if a woman says... "You know I think I've put on a few pounds in the last week", how does she expect her friends to respond? If she considers them to be 'good' friends, then they will say things like:

> *"Get away, you're as slim as ever."*
>
> *"Don't be silly now, of course you haven't."*

However, if she really has put on weight, then it could be argued that these are not the sort of responses that genuine friends should make. Real friends don't tell you what you *want* to hear, but what you *need* to hear.

Remember, we live in the real world of pretence, disillusion and pretension, often intended to protect people's fragile egos, so she certainly wouldn't expect, or want to be met with silence, for her friends to awkwardly avert their eyes, or for one of them to abruptly change the subject! If they do, then they won't remain friends for long.

Some people openly criticise themselves just so they can hear others vehemently reject this self-effacement. You may have come across this shallow characteristic in some people. In this case the woman may simply want to hear her friends say how slim she is; in effect it's a harmless way of inviting compliments to make her feel better.

By the way, don't *EVER* make the mistake I made many years ago when a girlfriend asked me if I thought her bum looked big in a skirt she was trying on. My reply was along the lines of... 'Well it does look a *bit* big, but only a bit.' I'll let you imagine what happened next, and I guess that explains why she very quickly became my ex-girlfriend!

Another, more recent example was seen on the popular T.V. show 'The Apprentice', when at dinner one evening a female contestant announced to her colleagues... "I can't believe Sir Alan said I was domineering. I'm not domineering, am I?"

The averted eyes and complete silence around the dinner table said it all!

The key point is that what's *not* said can often be more powerful and incisive than what *is* said. There are some things that people definitely do not expect you to say, my example above being a case in point. There are other things that people *do* expect you to say, or at least to respond to. Hence, when you don't respond in the way that they expect, or you don't respond at all, you can cut the air with a knife.

| | |
|---|---|
| Provocateur: | *"Graham is one of the most political people in this office, don't you agree?"* |
| Response 1: | [Silence]<br>"Can we get back to discussing the project plan? |
| Provocateur: | [In a group setting] *"I think we could solve this problem in one go if we just sacked the Board of Directors."* |
| Response 2: | [Silence]<br>"Thanks for that Derek. Now, does anyone have any suggestions of a more practical nature?"<br>*or...* and this one's even more in jest... |
| Response 3: | "Derek, I see that you've chosen this special moment to embarrass yourself in public... again!" |

Okay, you might want to don armour before you try the last one, but the point remains. When you want to register your disagreement without openly saying so, try these more subtle tactics and notice the results you get.

| | |
|---|---|
| **Counter tactics:**<br> | Use silence. |
| | Ignore the comment completely. |
| | Change the subject. |
| | Use humour. |
| | Use ridicule (but retain a sense of humour). |

So far we've discussed how you can challenge the specificity of statements, the frequency or last time that something happened, the accuracy of exaggerated labels and the power of what you don't say.

Let's now build on this to learn some more linguistic counter tactics to crimes of our time. Let's learn how to deal with a more direct, 'in your face' assault.

## Crime #5: Direct, Open Criticism

NB: We will return to this subject in Chapter 9 when we take the gloves off in dealing with direct insults and verbal abuse; but for now...

Imagine that the woman with the 'weight problem' is not referring to herself, but is instead directing this at you.

Provocateur:     *"Have you put on a few pounds recently?"*

How might you respond to this if it were directed at you?

- Embarrassment

- Anger

- Denial (whilst pulling your tummy in at the same time)

- Lash out at her for being so bloody rude

- Accuse her of being less than svelte herself. In fact, come to think of it, she makes Russell Grant look like a catwalk model!

Try this one on for size:

Response:       "Yes, but I'm finding it increasingly difficult to get up to my target weight of 280lbs. My personal coach says I've got to cut down on the celery and increase my Pop Tart and pepperoni intake, but it's so difficult. There's so much fresh fruit and vegetables around at this time of year."

What a stupid, and frankly ridiculous, response.                    Or is it?

Humour, when used skilfully, is one of the most effective stress and tension release mechanisms we have available. The response above is more 'strange' than funny, though its impact does rely upon the use of humour.

How does humour work and how can we use this to our advantage in such situations?

In simple terms, the structure of humour is based upon a 'surprise' ending to an otherwise predictable sequence of events. It's the unexpected change of tack that catches the listener by surprise and causes laughter, or in the example above, to throw the other person off track by responding in a way that they don't expect. This is the key.

For example, in an artist's studio one hears:

Artist:        *'Can I paint you in the nude?'*
Subject:     'I don't care what you wear!'

Or the old joke about the two nuns conversing in a shared bath:

Nun 1:      *"Where's the soap?"*

Nun 2:      "Yes it does, doesn't it"

Now, you didn't buy a corny old joke book, so let's get back to the point; how can we deflect direct criticism?

In the weight gain example the provocateur is trying to bait someone with a blatant insult. The response, which involves a combination of agreement, using the energy of the attack rather than fighting back, plus a healthy dose of humour, effectively derails the provocateur. By throwing them off track, it attempts to put the other person i.e. you, back in control.

---

**Counter Tactic:**      Choose to react in a way that they don't expect.

Use humour.

Show that you're completely un-fazed by any of this.

---

Here's another, typically derogatory comment, and one from which we can learn even more counter tactics.

Provocateur:      *"You're late!"*

Before you read on, stop and think about how you might respond to this accusation if it were shot at you as you entered a meeting room full of people? What would your typical, natural default response be, both verbally and behaviourally? In the real world we can only react in the moment to unanticipated events, so how would you react in this particular moment?

One possible response is to stumble towards the first vacant seat, hyperventilating and sweating, wildly scanning the assembled attendees whilst apologising profusely for delaying matters. You might lower yourself gingerly into the chair in a conciliatory fashion, hunch forwards, hug your knees and rock rhythmically back and forth.

Okay, maybe that's a bit of an exaggeration (Crime # 3).

Another, more professional response might be to say in a very 'level-headed' manner:

Response:        "You're right. I've been delayed by a few minutes."

**Analysis:**

This reply achieves several things in one hit:

- It re-directs the focus away from a negative judgement (being late) into a less emotive, factual concept (time); you're now talking about 'moments in 'time' not a 'monumental crime'.

- It reduces the severity of the event by putting it into perspective, i.e. just a few minutes, not hours or days, so what's the big deal?

- By refusing to argue, make excuses or fight back (which would probably make things worse), the accuser's attack is diffused.

- The brevity of your response signals the end of that particular interchange.

- You imply that you have also been inconvenienced, i.e. the delay is a result of something that happened to you rather than some act of negligence, disorganisation or sloppiness on your part.

Here's an alternative response to the same accusation:

| | |
|---|---|
| Provocateur: | *"You're late!"* |
| Response 2: | "Well, I'm not late now. If I don't show up for 24 hours, then you'll *really* know I'm late." |

## Analysis:

This is dangerous and childish, and if the provocateur is your boss it's almost certainly career limiting! However, there are things we can learn from this also:

· 'A few minutes delay' appears insignificant in the grand scheme of things, i.e. in relation to what 'seriously late' would look like – you're putting things into a broader context and wider perspective – something we touched on in Chapter 5.

· You're refusing to be baited or cowed by the assertion, the sub-text being 'Well I'm here now so let's not spend any more time arguing about it, let's get on with what we're here to do.'

And one more:

| | |
|---|---|
| Provocateur: | *"Storming out of the meeting like that was totally unacceptable."* |
| Response: | "I was frustrated by our lack of progress." |

## Analysis:

This reply:

· Again gives a level-headed, non-emotional factual response

· Side steps the criticism; can you 'feel' the side step as you read the response?

- Turns the described behaviour into a positive, i.e. if no progress is being made, then simply going around in circles is a waste of everyone's time
- Dilutes conflict-ridden expressions such as 'storming out' by replacing them with a less emotive word; in this case 'frustrated'.
- Refuses to rise to the bait by ignoring the judgemental part of the statement, i.e. that it is 'totally unacceptable'.

 **Exercise:**

See if you can come up with 'emotion reducing' responses to each of these accusations:

Provocateur:            *"You're sloppy."*

Provocateur:            *"He attacked me in the meeting."*

Provocateur:            *"She dominated the discussion."*

Provocateur:            *"You're not a team player."*

Provocateur:            *"He railroaded that decision."*

Provocateur:            *"You smoke too much."*

| Counter tactics:  | Use and quote the facts – this is the safest ground of all as no one can criticise you for being biased, prejudiced, manipulative or un-truthful when you stick to the facts. |
| --- | --- |
| | Subtly change emotion-laden labels into other less evocative expressions, e.g. 'horrendous' into 'unpleasant', 'fat' into a 'fuller figure', 'panicking' becomes 'concerned', 'concerned' becomes 'conscious of' and 'arguing' morphs into 'debating' etc. |
| | Work with the energy of the other person by not openly disagreeing with them. |
| | Contextualise your position within a bigger frame e.g. a longer time frame or wider sequence of other events. |
| | Refuse to be baited. |

So, moving on from dealing with unfair judgements about other people or situations… what do we do when others compound confusion by deciding in their own minds what a particular behaviour means?

This is a crime on top of a crime.

This is repeat offending.

## Crime #6: Making Connections Where None Exist

Taking the example of being accused of being 'late', let's now add an extra sting:

Provocateur:      *"You're late. Clearly, you don't see this as important!"*

Response:         "Yes, I've been delayed, but that's got nothing to do with how seriously I take this meeting."

Take a moment to analyse this reply, as you have done with the others, and take note of what you notice.

**Analysis:**

In addition to diffusing the language and agreeing that there's been a delay, this response:

- Openly challenges the provocateur's assertion that 'being late' automatically *means* 'not caring'
- Goes further by actively stating that the two concepts are unrelated.

Again, we see an example of working *with* the energy of the attack, and of changing emotive words into less-inflammatory ones. However, the critical distinction here is that the provocateur has committed a more serious crime by making an assumed link between two separate concepts. The connection may indeed be real, however, it could equally be something they've created in their own mind, and which they wish to propagate because it suits their purpose. In short, there could be no connection whatsoever between the two ideas, other than in their own limited view of reality.

In simple terms, the provocateur has decided that 'late' means 'you don't see this as important'. In verbally challenging this, you're questioning a potentially fictitious link. As a general principle, you refuse to accept at face value that one thing *automatically means* another.

Here's another example:

Provocateur:   *"You missed my birthday party. Clearly, you don't care about me."*

Response:   "Don't I usually come to your Birthday and other parties?"

Provocateur:   *"Normally, yes."*

Response 1:   "Okay, so why should you suddenly assume that because I missed it this time it means I don't care about you?"

**Analysis:**

· This response puts one event into the perspective of many similar events, the subtext being... 'You're blowing this out of proportion by picking on one exceptional occurrence.'

Here's another reply to the same provocation:

Provocateur:   *"You missed my birthday party. Clearly, you don't care about me."*

Response 2:   "Yes, I did miss your birthday and I'm very sorry about that. Putting birthdays aside for a moment, in what ways *do* I show that I care about you?"

**Analysis:**

This reply:

· Turns the tables by acknowledging the behaviour, 'missing the party', and then shifting attention to the accusation of 'not caring'; after all it's the 'not caring' aspect that's the issue. By challenging a much larger, broader and more substantial matter, you shift the focus away from perceived symptoms and on to their deeper meaning. All of this keeps you in control and puts the pressure back on the other party.

- Challenges the provocateur to give examples that disprove their own accusation. If they do give examples then they negate what they just said. If they don't give examples, then you can provide several of your own. Either way, you're back in control.

- Reveals recent examples that demonstrate that you really do care, which exposes the flaw in their logic, and questions how else and where else they

  may be using warped thinking.

Here's a couple of really powerful questions that you can use:

Response 3:     "Have there been times when I've showed up for something but you knew that I didn't really care at that time?"

Response 4:     "Is it possible that some of the people who come to your parties are just superficial friends; how many of them would really stand by you in a crisis, for example?"

Again, by asking for, or giving, counter examples, you're breaking the assumed connection between 'showing up', 'caring' or 'not caring'. This is about finding the exception, or exceptions that break the rule. However, in perpetrating the crime in the first place, the provocateur is trying to create a rule from just one exception. They've now been hoisted by their own petard.

Touché!

> *"One swallow does not a summer make."*
>
> William Shakespeare
>
> *"One swallow does not a drunkard make."*
>
> Jon Lavelle

## The 'Power of Three' Technique

The principle of challenging an assertion from three different perspectives, as implied above, can be incredibly powerful. For example:

Provocateur: *"You don't buy me flowers; you don't love me anymore."*

In general terms, if you want to challenge this assertion fully, then you need to explore examples where:

- 'A' (buying flowers) does not automatically mean 'B' (that you love someone)

- The absence of 'A' (i.e. no flowers) does not mean the opposite of 'B' (i.e. that you do *not* love them)

- The presence of 'B' (loving someone) does not automatically mean that it causes 'A' (the buying of flowers).

It can take a while to get your head around this, and it's common to have to re-read the above three statements in order to cement understanding. However, the 'Power of Three' technique is so fundamentally important that I'm going to give a couple more examples of how to use this three-point counter strategy.

Provocateur: *"You weren't saying much in the meeting; you don't seem to have a strong opinion either way on the matter."*

Response 1: "Sorry? Why does my lower share of air time in the meeting automatically mean that I don't have strong opinions on the matter?"

Response 2: "Do all people who are vocal in meetings necessarily have strong or useful opinions to offer?"

Response 3:     "Are all the quiet people in meetings less vocal simply because they have no opinion?"

And a more 'earthy' example, just for the ladies:

Provocateur:     *"All men are bastards!"*

Response 1:     "How does being a man automatically make them a 'bastard'?"

Response 2:     "Have you ever met a man who wasn't a 'bastard'?"

Response 3:     "Do you know any women who behave like that?"

So, in summary, to deal with situations where a person is making an unjustifiable or overly forced connection between two separate things you can respond with the 'Power of Three' technique, and add in some counter-examples of your own for good measure:

The 'Power of 3' is a potent rhetorical device that's used in many aspects of communication and influence. Here's just one example from the opening scene of Shakespeare's *Hamlet*.

## Three witches:

> *"When shall we three meet again?*
> *In thunder, lightning, or in rain?*
> *When the hurly-burly's done*
> *When the battle's lost and won*
> *That will be ere the set of sun."*

I could paraphrase, thus:

> "When shall ye use the 'Power of Three' again?
> In wonder, or enlightening an unjustified claim?
> When the twisted words are spun
> When the argument's lost and won
> That will be when the balance is re-won."

I digress; here are the key counter tactics for Crime #6:

| **Counter tactics:** | Show how 'A' does not automatically mean 'B' by: |
|---|---|
| | - Asking for examples of where we find 'A' but not 'B' |
| | - Asking for examples of where we find 'B' without 'A' |
| | - Giving examples yourself |
| | Use counter questions such as: |
| | - *"I know that you believe that A means B; but could you consider the possibility that it might mean C, D, or E?"* |
| | - *"That's interesting. What else could A mean?"* |

 **Exercise:**

Try the 'Power of Three' technique yourself using the provocations below. I've given just a few possible answers to the first example.

Provocateur:    *"Gavin's all red in the face, he must be angry."*

Answer:    "Yes, he could be angry, but he also....

- "Could be hot."

- "Could be embarrassed."

- "Might have just run upstairs."

- "Might have had an accident with food colouring in the kitchen!"

Now it's your turn; think of at least two possible alternative meanings for each of the following statements:

Provocateur:        *"Leaving the party early means he doesn't like us."*

Provocateur:        *"You're clearly avoiding me, you ignored me in Tesco's."*

Provocateur:        *"I'll never be a good mother, I can't even look after myself."*

Provocateur:        *"I'm late because of you."*

Provocateur:        *"The team lost the match because of the incompetence of the referee."*

Provocateur:        *"The team won because of the pep talk I gave them before kick-off."*

By now you should be starting to find suitable responses yourself, and remember there's always more than one.

It's amazing to realise just how many different replies you can give to such simple everyday statements. Maybe you've already begun to realise that you no longer have to accept what other people say at face value, and that there are far more elegant responses than simply arguing back, getting in a huff, storming off or swearing at someone. Sadly, these crude actions are automatic defaults for many people. However, you now have far more options available in your kit bag.

Let's take a look at the next crime to illustrate another set of linguistic detection tools.

## Crime #7: Using 'Universal Statements'

How often have you heard expressions such as:

*"You can never rely on him."*

*"She's always in a bad mood."*

*"The place will be empty."*

*"Nobody's perfect."*

*"There's always tomorrow."*

*"Nobody gives a toss around here."*

Okay, the fourth and fifth expressions are pretty harmless, and are actually quite uplifting, whilst the last is downright confrontational and defeatist in nature. However, if you want to challenge statements like this in the future, then there's a simple and effective way to do this, but first...

 **Health Warning**

Be careful, as with all the counter tactics in this chapter, if you over use one technique, then you become predictable, and it loses its power. Also, people will start to avoid you as you increasingly come across as a clinically cold and heartless beast!

Getting back to the examples above, they're all 'partners in crime' that we can group together as they collectively illustrate the same category of warped and dysfunctional thinking.
Here are some more:

*"You're always letting me down."*

*"Everyone agrees."*

*"I've never had a good meal there yet."*

*"Nobody's got a good word to say about him."*

What do you notice about all of these statements? What's the *universal* crime that each of them commits?

Okay, I've given you a clue in the question itself. They all deal in 'absolutes' such as 'always', 'never', 'everyone', 'nobody' etc. Absolutes are 100% or 0% statements, black or white in which there appear to be no exceptions or shades of grey. Of course, the analogue world in which we live is rarely so absolute, not least when dealing with personal opinion, subjective experiences, incomplete information, politics and downright bias.

So, the response to the following provocation gives you a simple, yet highly effective counter tactic that you can apply in similar situations in the future.

Provocateur:      *"Everybody knows that she's useless."*

Response:         *"Everybody? Do you really mean everybody?"*

The emphasis that I've indicated by underlining the three words above is deliberate and is a *required* part of your verbal response. You emphasise that you are unconvinced by their assertion, through the tonality and accenting of your response.

## Analysis:

The six words of this counter-challenge do at least four things; they:

· Question the universality of the statement, i.e. exposing the claim that absolutely everyone in the whole world knows or thinks something. This is patently ludicrous, other than with indisputable facts such as the Earth's round, we will all die one day and Father Christmas likes mince pies.

- Stop the person in their tracks as they now have to go back and justify why this is true in every case. They will almost always retract or modify their claim as they know it's an exaggeration that cannot be substantiated.

- Expose the unrealistic exaggeration, and imply that the provocateur has lost a sense of proportion or is no longer in touch with reality.

- Expose them for being manipulative or untruthful.

The simplest and most effective response you can make to universal statements is simply to challenge their universality. Using the detective work that you carried out for crime #6, you've now learned the technique of using at least three different perspectives. Let's take one of the other examples above to illustrate three different responses:

Provocateur:     *"I've never had a good meal there yet."*

Response 1:      "What, '*never*'? Do you *really* mean '*never*'?"

Response 2:      "That's interesting. I've heard good reports about the food from other people."

Response 3:      "What a shame. I've had several good meals there. Perhaps you've just been unlucky."

The first response challenges their experience, the second compares it with the experiences of others, and the third counters it with your own culinary encounters.

The example itself is not important; it's the principle that it illustrates. In all cases you're challenging the universality of their statement, and the more perspectives from which you do this, the more their assertion will wobble.

Here are three more possible examples based upon the same restaurant scenario:

Provocateur:       *"I've never had a good meal there yet."*

Response 4:        "Well there's obviously something good about the place or you wouldn't keep going back there would you?"

                   (Subtext – Are you stupid?)

                   [Hidden text – You *are* stupid!]

Response 5:        "Well they're clearly doing something right, it always seems pretty busy to me."

                   (Subtext – Maybe you're too fussy?)

                   [Hidden text – You're weird!]

Response 6:        "Did you do something to upset them on an earlier visit?"

                   9Subtext – Perhaps they're getting back at you for some reason; maybe you should be worried about what's going on; maybe you're a difficult customer?)

                   [Hidden text – They may be putting foreign bodies or some other distasteful substance in your soup! ... *Ugh!]*

So, let's summarise the universal counter tactics that we can use to challenge universal statements.

---

| | |
|---|---|
| **Counter tactics:**  | Challenge the universality of the statement by asking questions such as: |
| | - *"Everybody? Seriously?* You mean *absolutely everybody?"* |
| | - *"Nobody?* – what, not a *single person?"* |
| | - *"Always?* So there have never been *any* exceptions?" |
| | Use the 'Power of Three' technique |

Right, we've got one final crime on our hands to solve so…

> … *NOBODY* leaves the room

Oops, you see how easy it is for us to fall into the Universal Statement trap.

## Crime #8: Giving Non-Attributed Opinions

Okay, Sherlock Holmes, what's the crime being committed below?

Provocateur:     *"People are saying that she's useless."*

What's the very first word that you'd want to 'bring in' for further questioning?

Again, the answer's within my question because it is indeed the very first word… 'people'; and we might then challenge this with:

Response 1:     *"People?* When you say '*people*', who *exactly* is saying she's useless?"

## Analysis:

This response:

- Refuses to accept opinions from un-named individuals as being valid.

- Forces the provocateur to name individuals, which puts them in a defensive position, particularly if these people are few in number or, even more tellingly, if they don't exist at all! It happens; and that's partly why myths and rumours originate and propagate.

- Seriously undermines the provocateur's position if they refuse to name who these 'mystery people' are. From your perspective, how are you expected to believe anything when you don't know who it is you're being asked to believe?

- Exposes the provocateur as either a subversive gossip, a highly political animal or a blatant liar. I guess you could always give them the opportunity to save face by letting them choose which most appropriately applies from the above list!

What's happening in this scenario is that one individual is projecting their *own* opinion on to a whole heap of 'other people'. They're seeking to build the strength of their case by effectively saying "Well it's not just me, it's a whole bunch of 'people' who've come to this very same conclusion."

By attributing an opinion to an un-named group of people the speaker is seeking to establish their own opinion as undisputed fact, using the tenuous principles of 'strength in numbers, and the 'wisdom of crowds'.

Now their opinion may indeed be widely held, in which case perception matches reality. However, there are occasions when it patently isn't true and the provocateur is maliciously trying to bad-mouth, or otherwise discredit another person by spreading myths, injustices and untruths. These comments are more easily propagated if they're attributed to 'anonymous, multiple others'... unless of course they're challenged.

But wait, we're not done yet. You can go further by forcing the provocateur to come out from behind their anonymous human shield and to state their *own* opinion. By using this tactic you challenge them to take personal responsibility for the slur, as in:

Response 2:   "So what do *you* think? Do *you* say she's useless?" I'm interested in *your* opinion."

**Analysis:**

This response:

- Forces the provocateur to take ownership for the opinion, as opposed to hiding behind what other (un-named) people supposedly think or have said

- Enables you to discount the opinion as unsubstantiated unless the provocateur is prepared to stand by it themselves, or can provide evidence from elsewhere

- Completely destroys the allegation if they state that this is *not* their opinion, as it's then neither true for you nor for them. You are then only left with the supposed, unsubstantiated opinion of others, with which you *both* now disagree!

Hurrah!

Here's another example, which illustrates an alternative counter tactic:

Provocateur:   *"You don't work hard enough."*

Whose opinion do you think this is? It's more than likely the opinion of the provocateur, and if so, you can use this fact as part of your countering tactic, as in:

Response 3:          "In *your* opinion."

**Analysis:**

This response:

- Is quite confrontational as it attempts to isolate the individual, along with their personal opinion
- Implies that it is only the provocateur who holds the opinion
- States that their opinion is only that, i.e. an opinion, which is not the same as an established fact
- Is likely to lead to an escalation of the argument! ☹

Remember, not all of the techniques available to us will work in every case, and some have more potential to inflame the situation rather than to calm it. However, it would be remiss not to highlight the full range of options available as they could easily be used on you, so it's best to be aware.

It's up to you to choose from this armoury, and to apply the techniques in an intelligent manner. With this in mind, here are two further examples which illustrate additional counter tactics.

Provocateur:          *"You should go to church."*

Which of the five words above strikes you as being value-laden?

Please think about this now before reading further.

It's the word 'should', because within it lies a thinly disguised opinion. There's a toxic family of similar words that contain some element of value-laden opinion or a value-judgement, including:

> "You have to…"
>
> "You must…"
>
> "You're expected to…"
>
> "You need to…"
>
> "You won't be able to…"
>
> "You won't be allowed to…"
>
> "You're supposed to…"
>
> "You ought to…"

Whenever you hear expressions such as these be careful, as they're potentially dangerous if taken at face value. Let's now respond to the above provocation:

Provocateur:      *"You should go to church."*

Response 4:      "What would happen if I didn't?"

**Analysis:**

This response:

- Uses the technique of 'considering the opposite' which we referred to in Chapter Five.
- Directly challenges the assertion that a certain thing has to happen, by opening up the possibility that it won't.
- Challenges the universality of the statement.

- Puts the provocateur on the defensive, as they have to both struggle with the fact that you're likely to oppose their assertion, whilst at the same time having to justify why the assertion is valid.

And finally:

Provocateur:     *"Everyone on welfare is lazy."*

Response 5:      "Have you ever been on welfare? If so, were you lazy?"

                 *or*

Response 6:      "I was on welfare once; are you saying *I'm* lazy?"

If you want to be particularly 'naughty' you could invent the last one on the basis that you are using a 'white lie' to counter a much more serious crime.

A few weeks ago I was in Tesco's at the checkout, and outside I could hear a dog barking. The barking had been going on for some time, and as the checkout operator scanned my goods he said... "That dog's an absolute pain, someone should take proper control of it. The owner's clearly not trained it properly as it barks at everyone."

As I was in the mood for having a bit of fun with him, I simply replied in a very calm manner:

"It's my dog."

I couldn't have had more impact on the checkout operator if I'd thrown a bucket of water over him. He immediately started to back-track on his assertion, apologising profusely, and digging himself into an even bigger hole as he then started saying that he was sure that the dog was really nice, and was probably just being excited or provoked by passing customers.

Now before you start to think that I really shouldn't play such 'cruel' games on people like this, I should point out that it really was my dog. He's called Frazier, and he's never harmed anyone or anything in his life. He's just rather fond of barking. I'm not sure which is the greater social nuisance; the dog barking at passers by, or the checkout operator barking out unsubstantiated opinions to complete strangers?

You decide.

---

**Counter tactics:**

Challenge non-attributed opinions with questions such as:

- "*People*? When you say '*people*', who exactly is saying he doesn't work hard enough?"

- "So what do *you* think? Do *you* say she needs to improve her dress sense?"

- "According to *whom*?"

Other techniques:

- "In your opinion."

- "What would happen if I didn't?"

Turn the tables by applying the slur or opinion to the speaker, someone else you know or yourself, as in:

- "Have you ever been on welfare? If so, were *you* lazy?"

- "My mother once found herself having to rely on welfare as a result of my father walking out on us; it was a very difficult time for all of us, especially the younger ones, but she worked her fingers to the bone to keep the family home together."

- "I was once on welfare; are you calling *me* lazy?"

**Exercise:**

Time for some mental gymnastics. It's over to you now as we test whether what we've covered in this chapter has begun to equip you with the skills to effectively counter the most common linguistic crimes and misdemeanours of wrongful thinking.

So, as I've thrown some pretty 'heavy' material at you in this chapter, I'm going to end on a light-hearted note, and hopefully with a bit of fun.

Here's some good old-fashioned silly humour, from Monty Python!

## 'Monty Python and the Holy Grail'

Fans of Monty Python, and in particular the cult movie '*Monty Python and the Holy Grail*', will fondly recall the scene in which a rowdy group of villagers bring forward to Bedevere, the village elder, a woman whom they suspect of being a witch!

I've reproduced a portion of the script overleaf, as in just this one scene it is possible to detect many of the 'crimes' that we've talked about in this chapter. Rather than point them out to you, my challenge is for you to now use this as a way of fine-tuning your perceptive skills by playing a game of 'spot the crime'.

The scene opens with Bedevere, the village elder and law-maker, standing on a stage in front of a large crowd of excited villagers.

Enjoy!

Villager:      We have found a witch; may we burn her?

Crowd:         *BURN HER... BUUUURN HER!*

Bedevere:      But how do you *know* she is a witch?

Villager:      She looks like one!

Other villager: Yeah!  She looks like one!!!

Bedevere:      Bring her forward.

[A young woman is pushed through the crowd of villagers to the platform. She is dressed all in black, has a carrot tied around her face on top of her nose, and a black paper witches hat on her head. She talks in a strange way because her nose is obscured by the carrot.]


Witch:         I'm *not* a witch, I'm *not* a witch!

Bedevere:      Er,... But you are *dressed* as one.

Witch:         *THEY* dressed me up like this.

Villagers:     No! Nooo!  We didn't!  We didn't!

Witch:         And this isn't my nose, it's a false one!

[Bedevere lifts up the carrot to reveal the woman's real 'normal-sized' nose]


Bedevere:      Well?

One villager:  Well, we did do the nose.

Bedevere:      The nose?

Villager:      And the hat. But she *is* a witch!

Villagers:     YEAH! BURN HER! BURN HER! BURN HER!

Bedevere:      Did you dress her up like this?

Villagers:     NO! No, No, No, No, No, No...

One villager:  Yes.

Villagers:     Yes. Yes. Yes.  A bit. Yes. A bit. A bit.

Villager:      Well, she *has* got a wart.

Bedevere:      What makes you think she is a witch?

Villager:      Well... she turned me into a newt!!

[Long Pause, incredulous look from Bedevere.]

Bedevere:     A *newt*?

[Long pause.]


Villager:     I got better...

Villagers:    *BURN HER anyway! BURN! BURN! BURN HER!*

Bedevere:     Quiet, quiet, quiet, QUIET. There are ways of telling whether she is a witch!

Villagers:    Are there?  What?  Tell us, then!  Tell us!

Bedevere:     Tell me... what do you do with witches?

Villagers:    *BUUUURN!!!!! BUUUUUURRRRNN!!!!!  You BURN them!!!!*

Bedevere:     And what do you burn apart from witches?

Villager:     More witches!

Other villager: Wood.

Bedevere:     So. Why do witches burn?

[Long silence. Shuffling of feet by the villagers.]


Villager:     Because they're made of... errr... wood?

Bedevere:     Goooood!

Villagers     Oh yeah...

[Obvious relief in getting the answer right]

Bedevere:     So, how do we tell whether she is made of wood?

One villager:  [Triumphantly]  Build a bridge out of her!

Bedevere:     Aah! But can you not also make bridges out of stone?

Villagers:    Oh yeah. Err... Umm...

Bedevere:     Does wood sink in water?

One villager:  No! No, no, it floats!

Other villager: Throw her into the pond!

Villagers:    YEEEAAAHHHH!

[When order is restored.]


Bedevere: What also floats in water?

| | |
|---|---|
| Villager 1: | Bread! |
| Villager 2: | Apples! |
| Villager 3: | Uh... very small rocks! |
| Villager 4: | Cider! |
| Villager 1: | Gravy! |
| Villager 3: | Cherries! |
| Villager 2: | Mud! |
| Villager 4: | Churches! Churches! |
| Villager 3: | Lead! Lead! |

[King Arthur steps into view.]

| | |
|---|---|
| King Arthur: | A Duck! |
| Villagers: | Ooooooh! |
| Bedevere: | Exactly! |

[Bedevere now turns to the rabble.]

| | |
|---|---|
| Bedevere: | So, logically...? |
| Villager: | If... she weighs the same as a duck... she's made of wood. |
| Bedevere: | And therefore...? |

[Pause.]

| | |
|---|---|
| Villager: | A Witch! |

[With ecstatic glee...]

All villagers: *A WITCH!*

If you haven't seen the film, then you should know that they do consequently weigh her using Bedevere's largest set of scales, and she does indeed weigh the same as the duck!

Well, that's Monty Python for you.

# Chapter 8

Perception, Meaning and Reality

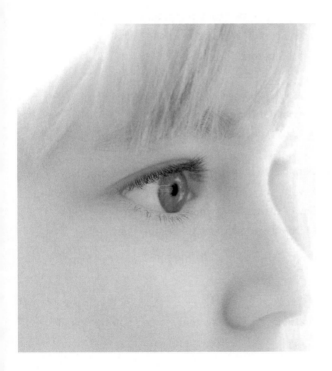

# 8 Perception, Meaning and Reality

How often do you scratch your head and wonder why people do what they do? "What's wrong with them... can't they see?"

Equally, how often have you done or said something, and not understood someone else's unexpected reaction? "What have I done? What on earth was it I said that made them react like that?"

> *"Before removing the splinter from your friend's eye;*
> *First remove the log from your own."*
>
> The Bible

What I take from this ancient quote is that it's a natural human tendency to think that the problem lies with the other party, or to expect other people to operate from the same view of the world as you do. However, we know that individuals perceive reality from their own, unique perspective.

In this chapter we will:

· Distinguish between perception and reality.

· Recognise that people do things for reasons that we don't always initially understand.

- Learn how to change the way in which we think about life's events, a process called 're-framing', which turns them into far more helpful views of the world.

- Continue our detective theme, by highlighting three common 'thought crimes', and learn how we can deal with each of these effectively.

When you look at an unmade bed do you see a hurried departure, a tangled mess, nothing unusual as it's how your bed looks all the time, the result of a night of unbridled passion, a naughty child's broken promise, or a great work of modern art?

Perhaps you see something else.

## 'Art' or 'Rubbish'?

Other people live in their own worlds, not in yours. Actually that's quire reassuring. More worryingly however, no-one lives in the 'real world', as they have their own internal representation of the world, their own world, in which they are the only inhabitants.

Before you think I've gone completely mad, consider that any reaction to my assertion that 'no-one lives in the real world', or indeed that 'there is no such thing as the 'real world', is a perfect illustration of what we're talking about. It's an example of how most readers will have viewed the world, up to this point.

One of the difficulties we face when interpreting the world around us is that what we know and experience 'inside ourselves' can differ radically from what exists 'outside ourselves'. We call the former 'human subjectivity', whereas the latter is 'reality'. However, as just stated, reality does not exist in, err... reality! It only exists in the billions of individual perceptions that humans have of what happens around them. Psychologists who want to use long words in order to confuse us might call this the 'collective conscious.'

This is not to say that perception cannot equal reality, because where incontrovertible facts are concerned then perception and reality are the same. However, problems rarely occur when the only things under discussion are absolute and quantifiable facts. It's all the other 'stuff' that causes us problems, and dealing in mere facts is child play. Here's a true, personal story that graphically illustrates my point.

## "How the Hell Could You Possibly Know?"

In 1994 I cycled across Ireland with my (then) best mate – ha ha! Everything was fine until he developed a problem with his left knee, which meant that cycling was quite painful for him. I was sympathetic, but he was determined that we press on, and as he was so insistent I agreed, as we had set ourselves goals for specific destination points at the end of each day.

A couple of days later I also developed a problem with one of my knees. It's interesting that neither of us had suffered from knee ailments in the past, but those are the circumstances in which we found ourselves, and we were now both cycling with painful knees, both intent on meeting our daily mileage targets.

Unfortunately, my friend refused to believe that I had a problem, or at least to accept that the pain that I was experiencing could even be approaching the excruciating agony that seared through his body with every turn of his pedals. I was in acute pain too, but of course there's no way of proving this to someone who's being irrational. (Sorry mate, if you're reading this, but I've got to set the record straight, and I made it into print before you did!)

Anyway, it all culminated in my friend telling me, with 100% conviction, that my pain could not be anything like as bad as his. I had now had enough, and told him in a 'flowery and expletive fashion' that there was no way on God's earth that he could possibly know how or what I was feeling in my knee, and that he could just f*** off.

This was on day 5 of a 9 day holiday. I don't know how we ever managed to complete the trip without an outburst of physical violence, but somehow we got home with nothing bruised other than our knees, our pride and our ego's.

It may or may not surprise you to learn, that it took more than four years before the emotional scars had healed sufficiently for us to resume our relationship; albeit from a very guarded, cagey, fragile and embarrassingly tentative stance.

| | |
|---|---|
| **Provocation** ☞ | "You don't see what I see; you can't see what I see. |
| | You don't feel exactly what I feel; you can't feel what I feel. |
| | By definition your perspective has to be different; you're standing in a different place. |
| | Oh yes... and you've got different knees!" |

So, getting back to my original question about art or rubbish; when you look at an exhibit at the Tate Modern gallery in London, such as Tracy Emin's 'Unmade Bed', or Carl Andre's 'Pile of Bricks', do you see modern art or a heap of old junk? Do you perceive the creator as a genius of art or a genius of con-artistry?

Are you the sort of person who tends to see jars that are half full or jars that have been half emptied by someone else? Do you look at the rain and think 'another wet and miserable day', or do you think 'how refreshing, think of the good this will do to the garden'?

Only today I heard on BBC Radio 4's weather forecast… "Unfortunately the Midlands are in for another wet and miserable day." Why automatically assume that rain is an unfortunate thing (it depends upon lots of things, including your personal situation and perspective), and even worse, why go further and dare to presume that 'wet' means 'misery'?

## If the 'Shoe' Fits…

There's an old tale, I don't even know if it is true, about a shoe salesman from Europe who visited Africa to investigate new markets for their products. After just a few days he sent a telex back to Head Office saying… 'Big mistake…We're wasting our time…No one wears shoes out here…Returning on the next boat…END.'

Undeterred, Head Office sent a second shoe salesman, before the first had returned, to see what he could find out. Immediately upon his arrival the second salesman excitedly telexed Head Office with these words… 'Great news…Massive market out here… No-one wears shoes…Send three container loads of shoes immediately…END.'

This phenomenon of differing, often polarised perceptions, is most cleverly depicted by the current series of HSBC poster advertisements. These show contrasting pairs of images with one-word descriptors attached to each image, immediately followed by the same pictures with the words interchanged. For example, one image shows a cricket match with the word 'Riveting' underneath, paired with a picture of a ballet dancer in action with the word 'Tedious' appended. Next to this are the same two pictures with the two words interchanged. The point is that both sets of images make sense, depending upon your perspective of how you feel about cricket and ballet.

HSBC in my view, are being extremely clever with these advertisements by using the technique of 'neurological shock', a series of provocative images and words that abruptly capture attention. One of the reasons why the images have such a dramatic effect is because many of the juxtaposed images and words jar with how some individuals have, hitherto, viewed the world. Because HSBC have paired two sets of images and words there's every chance that any viewer finds their neurones shocked.

## Sprouts, Malt Whisky and Blue Cheese

I now love sprouts, malt whisky and blue cheese. If you had asked me about any of these things 20 years ago, and in the case of blue cheese only three years ago, I would have told you that I would prefer to prise my fingernails off with pliers. Now I love all three... though I'm less keen when they're mixed together, as I found out only today when visiting my sister for lunch (it is Christmas Day 2007 as I write this). Perhaps I will feel differently in another 20 years time? I certainly hope I feel better tomorrow.

Anyway, we think in 'see-hear-feel-taste-smell' terms i.e. through our five major senses (assuming they're all working). In my example above the majority of information came to me through taste and smell, though the other senses played a secondary part. These are the five ways in which we perceive our environment, and of how we view ourselves within that space. From all of this we construct our personal 'map of the world'.

Clever stuff, this instant map-making, and you don't even need to consciously think about it. Hmmm... perhaps that's part of the problem.

Continuing the theme... consider the map of the London Underground. The map is only a representation of the tunnels and how the stations are connected. In fact, it's not even to scale or in relative proportion; it's merely a representation of reality. If you were to directly overlay a map of the London Underground onto a London street map, you would find that that they don't directly correlate.

Similarly, we all construct our own 'maps' of how we see the 'world' around us, and we carry these maps with us in our heads like a self-constructed Satellite Navigation System. If we metaphorically come up against a dead end, find ourselves in confusing territory, or encounter something that doesn't make sense, our default response is not to question our mental 'map', but rather to question the behaviour of other people. After all, 'It's not *us* that's got the problem, It's *other people*... isn't it? *We* know what's right; *they* clearly don't have a firm grasp on reality. They're using an out of date map, or the wrong map altogether.

What makes this fascinating, and the reason why the HSBC posters are so effective, is that each person's map of reality, how they perceive situations and events around them, is unique, and in some cases two people can have completely opposing views about what a situation means.

---

**Provocation**
  The 'map' is not the same as 'reality'.

---

**A Story**
The artist Pablo Picasso was travelling across Spain by train when he was recognised by another passenger, a businessman who was used to getting his own way, in business and life in general. After exchanging pleasantries, the

businessman told Picasso that whilst he admired the artist's success, he felt his paintings could be improved.

*"How so?"* replied the bemused Picasso.

*"Well,"* the businessman began, *"Your paintings are too abstract - you should paint things more as they really are."*

*"Could you explain more specifically what you mean?"* asked Picasso politely.

*"Certainly!"* the businessman replied, pulling a small photo from out of his wallet. *"Look at this photograph of my wife. This is how she actually looks - not some silly abstract representation."*

Picasso studied the photograph carefully for a few moments, and then asked... *"This is how your wife actually looks?"*

The businessman nodded proudly.

*"She's very small"* observed Picasso wryly.

Have you ever found yourself saying things like "I'm sorry, were we even in the same room together?" In other words you have a completely different perception of what happened or what you agreed in a prior meeting.

I'm sure we have all had this experience, so, how is it possible for two individuals to witness the same event and come away with such completely different points of view about what actually happened?

Here's an ancient Indian poem which gives us a clue:

# The Blind Men and the Elephant

It was six men of Indostan, to learning much inclined,
Who went to see the Elephant (Though all of them were blind),
That each by observation, might satisfy his mind

The First approached the Elephant, and happening to fall
Against his broad and sturdy side, at once began to bawl:
'God bless me! but the Elephant is very like a wall!'

The Second, feeling of the tusk, cried, 'Ho! what have we here?
So very round and smooth and sharp, to me 'tis mighty clear
This wonder of an Elephant is very like a spear!'

The Third approached the animal, and happening to take
The squirming trunk within his hands, thus boldly up and spake:
'I see,' quoth he; the Elephant is very like a snake!'

The Fourth reached out an eager hand, and felt about the knee
'What most this wondrous beast is like is mighty plain', quoth he;
'Tis clear enough the Elephant is very like a tree!'

The Fifth, who chanced to touch the ear, said: 'E'en the blindest man
Can tell what this resembles most; deny the fact who can
This marvel of an Elephant is very like a fan!'

The Sixth no sooner had begun about the beast to grope,
Than, seizing on the swinging tail that fell within his scope,
'I see,' quoth he, 'the Elephant is very like a rope!'

And so these men of Indostan, disputed loud and long,
Each in his own opinion exceeding stiff and strong,
Though each was partly in the right, and all were in the wrong!

John Godfrey Saxe

**Moral:**
> So oft in theological wars, the disputants ween,
> Rail on in utter ignorance of what each other mean,
> And prate about an Elephant, not one of them has seen!

———————————————

Personal evaluations such as... "The fish course was excellent" or "The lead actor was pathetic", are private human activities that only occur in the mind.

So, nothing actually 'is'. Our reality exists within our own minds, and other people's reality exists within theirs. Both perceived realities could be different and correct, at the same time. I thought the fish dish was excellent, you thought it tasted like a two day old nappy. Who's right? The answer is both of us; and you should see my knees!

Also, things change with time, so what was strange and inexplicable in 2005, can be regarded as normal behaviour in 2010. Just as what is unspeakable behaviour in Stockholm, and which will quickly get you arrested, is everyday, expected behaviour in Los Angeles, and in fact, if you don't engage in such activities you're regarded as weird.

So do people not know better?

No, they often don't, because they don't see the things the way that we see them; and yes, they often do know better, because they see things that we do not see.

I will conclude this section with an amusing scenario, which again illustrates the phenomenon of differing perceptions.

## In the psychiatrist's chair

In the psychiatric world there is a famous perception test called the 'Rorschach Test', better known as the 'Ink Blot Test'.

The psychiatrist takes a piece of clean white paper and drips a few drops of black ink on it. They then fold the paper in half, so that the ink spreads out across both sides of the inner face of the paper. On opening up the sheet a random symmetrical ink blot shape is revealed, and the idea is that the patient should then describe what they see. The theory being that they will only 'see' what they want to see, and in disclosing what they perceive, they inadvertently give away some of their inner perceptions, compulsions, prejudices and fixations.

So, the doctor opens the folded sheet and asks his subject what he sees? The patient studies it for a moment and then describes some pornographic scene, in considerable detail. "Hmm" says the psychiatrist. "Let's try a different one." Again the psychiatrist performs the experiment with a new sheet of paper and a new ink blot. "What do you see now?" he enquires. The man looks at the second ink blot and this time describes some lurid scene involving a couple of lesbian lover". "I see..." remarks the Doctor. "And what do you see in this third image?" This time the man gasps, and with some embarrassment describes an orgy of the most outlandish proportions, and in the most graphic detail.

"It's clear to me", said the doctor, folding the papers and putting them to one side, "That you have a sexual obsession of the highest order."

"*DON'T BLAME ME!*", protests the patient... "*You're the one with the dirty pictures!*"

Perception... and reality; it's all within the eye of the beholder.

We will now go on to explore how this can help explain why people appear to do strange things.

## People Make the Best Choices they Can, at the Time

Have you been in a situation where you did the 'wrong' thing, yet at the time you were simply trying to do the very best you could? You might have been trying to help someone, for example guiding an old lady across the road, but ended up making things worse... when you realised that she didn't want to cross in the first place!

In relation to your own well-intentioned situations, if you'd had a better choice open to you in each instance, would you not have taken it? After all, if it's a 'better choice' then why would you not have taken that route?

With the possible exception of suicide victims and self-harmers, who knowingly make decisions that will hurt them, recognising this human flaw helps us to view these actions from a different perspective.

> **Provocation**
>
> All behaviour has a positive intention.

Every human behaviour has a purpose and is useful in some context. It is when behaviour is exhibited in the 'wrong' context that problems arise. A topless woman on the beach in Nice goes un-noticed, whereas if she were to remove her blouse and bra as she walked down the High Street in Henley-on Thames she would be arrested; though hopefully not *too* quickly, eh gents!

Punching someone in the face at a business meeting might be perceived as a little over-zealous, whereas, if the perpetrator did this to a person who was trying to mug an old lady, again in the High Street in Henley-on Thames, then it would be seen as an act of heroism by most, but not all people, as the mugger, his friends and family may see things differently.

Incidentally, a lot happens in Henley-on Thames High Street; you should go there some day.

So, if we accept that people make the best choices open to them when they act, (even the mugger was trying to achieve something positive for himself), then before we jump to (the wrong) conclusions, we should first try to understand the *purpose* behind another's 'inappropriate' behaviour.

If you get to the root cause of the behaviour then this will always reveal a 'positive' intention.

What could be the positive intentions at the very heart of these behaviours?

· The woman who attempts suicide

· The man who smacks his child

· The boss who gives you negative feedback

· The man who sends hate mail

· The woman who hates males

If you think about situations such as this hard enough you will uncover a possible reason why a person might act in this way that indicates a positive intention on their part, or you will think of a context, situation or time in which it could be the right thing to do.

It's a question of what a behaviour 'means' to you when and where you observe it.

## What Does Anything Mean?

Cognitive psychologists have suggested that at some level, people respond to life's events and circumstances with two simple questions:

1. What does this mean?

2. Given that meaning, what is my best response to this event or circumstance?

However, as we've already discovered, events can have multiple meanings.

For example, if someone tells you that their partner's left them, most people would assume that they're going to be sad for a while and then move on, and if that's your interpretation you'll respond accordingly, with a blend of sympathy and encouragement.

But what else could it mean?

· Now they're free to meet someone who's *really* right for them.

· They'll never meet anyone else and they'll be alone, and miserable, for the rest of their lives (Notice, how in this example, as in the weather forecast, a 'meaning' has been attached to being alone).

· What they learn from the experience will make them a more loving partner in the future.

· That's it; they're scarred for life and will never experience love again .

· It's an opportunity to fight to win their partner back.

· There's something wrong with them, something we're not being told.

· It's life's way of saying 'time to move on'.

· Wow, how lucky can you get? Now you're free to play the field again!

After a few rounds of this game it becomes clear that it's possible to make up numerous different meanings for any given event, and a new, even more useful question emerges which is… "What do you *want* this to mean?"

> *"When I use a word," Humpty Dumpty said in rather a scornful tone,*
> *"It means just what I choose it to mean - neither more nor less."*

> *"The question is," said Alice, "whether you can make words*
> *mean so many different things?"*
>
> - Lewis Carroll

So, picking up on the theme of Chapter Five (Options, Choices, Control and Thinking), why not choose what you want things to mean?

---

**Tactic:**  Choose what you want things to mean.

---

As you begin consciously choosing the meanings you apply to the events and circumstances of your life, you will be able to create more effective answers to the question of how best to respond to them.

> *"Flexibility comes from having multiple choices;*
> *Wisdom comes from having multiple perspectives."*
>
> - Robert Dilts

While at first glance this may seem an innocuous idea, its implications are far reaching. For example, how might you behave differently if you recognised that the person who is voting for a different candidate to you in the local or national election is not a moronic idiot but rather someone who's making their best judgement based upon their narrow perspective on a wider picture?

How might you behave differently if you recognized that people, including yourself, are physiologically incapable of seeing the whole picture all at once, and that the art of gathering multiple perspectives is both a skill that needs to be consciously cultivated and a necessary part of effective decision-making?

So how do we do this? How do we go about choosing what things mean and cementing these into our reality?

It's called 'frame-changing'.

## Frame Changing

> *"That's much nicer Jon...*
> *Now that you've gone and put a nice frame around it."*
>
> Jon's Mum

Just as a picture takes on a new look, depending upon the frame that you put around it, the same is true of how we choose to perceive, or to 'frame' events.

Re-framing does exactly what it says on the tin; it puts a new psychological frame around an event or situation. When you re-frame your perspective you change the *meaning* in a situation; you will see things differently, in a new light, and as a result you're likely to experience different emotions. For example:

Provocateur:          *"That's disgusting."*

Does this thing, that's 'disgusting', stand alone? No, everything is 'something' within a context, so in what context is the thing disgusting? Could it actually be 'entertaining' in a different context, for example if performed as part of a comedy routine?

As we've learned throughout this book, the real world is often more complicated than people seek to portray it. Black or white are rarely the only options, there are many shades of grey in-between, and usually more options than a simple "Yes" or "No".

There's a great little exercise that I learned many years ago from Richard Bandler, the co-founder of NLP (Neuro Linguistic Programming), called 'The Sunny Side of the Street'. I've reproduced it here so that you can get some practice in re-framing.

 **Exercise**

Take each of the statements below and re-frame them into a positive interpretation. For example:

Statement 1:  *"I pay too much tax."*

Re-frame:  "Wow, that must mean that you earn a lot of money."

Statement 2:  *"My mother-in-law is so nosey."*

Re-frame:  "It must be nice to know that she cares enough about you to take such an interest in your life."

Have some fun with this, and challenge yourself not to read on until you have come up with at least one positive re-frame for each of the following:

Statement 3:      *"My Son has left home – the house is so empty nowadays."*

Your Re-frame:

Statement 4:      *"It's raining again."*

Your Re-frame:

Statement 5:      *"I've been up all night with diarrhoea and vomiting."*

Your Re-frame:

Statement 6:      *"That's the fortieth publisher that's turned my book down."*

Your Re-frame:

Statement 7:      *"The Doctor said that I'm developing Alzheimers."*

Your Re-frame:

Statement 8:      *"Freddy Starr ate my hamster."*

Re-frame:

---

**Tactics:**   Use re-framing to change what things mean.

Practice re-framing what others say.

Practice re-framing your own interpretation of what happens to you.

Play the 'Sunny Side of the Street' game at your next dinner party, or when friends come around. Each person, in turn, states a problem or issue of some kind, and the other guests then have to use their imagination to re-frame it in a positive light.

## Beware of Generalising, Distorting or Deleting

This section follows logically from the previous discussion as it focuses upon three common 'thought crimes'; the human tendency to generalise, distort, delete or to filter information.

Two key messages here are:

1. Limit how much you do these things, or at least be aware of what you're doing, and so retain a sense of control

2. Expose others, when you catch them doing these things in ways that are not helpful to either themselves or to others

Let me explain each of these three thought crimes in turn:

### 1.  What is 'Generalisation', and why do we do it?

We generalise in order to simplify the world, by categorising things, events and people. For example, at the simplest level, every time we encounter a handle on a door we don't think to ourselves… "What on Earth's this? What's it for? How does it work?" We know a door handle when we see one, even though there are thousands of different designs across the world. We just grab the thing' and twist it, pull it or push. Imagine how complicated it would be just getting through your day if every single encounter with door handles was a new learning experience; and that's just door handles!

So, this is an example of a *helpful* use of generalisation.

Another example of generalisation is when we group people together, or as we discussed in Chapter Seven, we label them. We might say that Jane's an Accountant or Adam's a Southerner. These may be accurate, harmless and helpful descriptions, but often such labels carry with them implicit, un-stated assumptions. It's common, for example, for people to associate Accountants with boring work, or even as being boring people. Earlier, we discussed how 'being alone' can be implicitly or explicitly linked with being 'miserable', for example.

Now before you accuse me of falling into my own traps, please ask yourself honestly if you think that in the Accountant example this is how a large number of people really do view such people? If so, then you've identified a widespread generalisation across society.

What about Adam being lumped into the ill-defined group of 'Southerners'? 'South of what?' would be my first question; South Uist, South London, or an inhabitant of Antarctica? Okay, I'm being silly now, but you get the point. What's of more concern are the implicit, negative associations that can accompany such generalisations, and in respect of some geographic regions the associations border on the libellous. What do you think of when you think of a man from Wales, a girl from Bangkok, a single middle-aged man who's just returned from holidaying alone in Thailand, or a mature lady who's lived all her life with her sister in Husband's Bosworth in Lincolnshire?

If we get into the territory of using even more emotive generalisations such as "Zahid's a Muslim fanatic", "Philip's a hard line Conservative" or "Susan's in with the 'swinging set", then we're potentially on more dodgy ground. Perhaps the rule here is to keep religion, politics and sex out of it, or at least not to combine all three at the same time!

So, these are examples of how people 'generalise'. We have to, just to function in today's information-laden society. The danger with generalisation is that we lose the specifics or nuances of a situation, and we potentially associate people with characteristics that are not accurate.

I was sitting in the First Class carriage of a train out of London last week when an unshaven bloke in a bright green pullover staggered in, clutching a can of Carlsberg Special Brew lager and an Aldi carrier bag. He sat down heavily opposite me, and continued to slurp from his can. When the ticket inspector arrived I handed over my 1st class ticket. The guy in the green sweater then handed over his 1st class ticket.

So, as a general rule (ha ha), be careful when you generalise, and watch out for how others can influence people and twist reality when they do so.

| Tactics: | Be aware of how, where and why you generalise – is it helping you or limiting your perception of the world? |
|---|---|
| | Be conscious of how others generalise, and in particular, don't let them get away with unhelpful, poisonous or damaging generalisations. |

## 2. What is 'Distortion', and why do we do it?

We distort information to fit our view of reality, again without realising, as beliefs, values, attitudes and perceptions come into play. We may see an individual's risqué jokes as playful or as deeply insulting depending upon our perspective. We perceive a tap on the arm as a sign of affection or even a 'come on', or we interpret it as an aggressive or personally intrusive act. Again, it depends upon how we choose to perceive the situation, and often... on *who's* doing the tapping!

As we learned from our re-framing exercise earlier, we can perceive an enquiry from our Mother-in-Law of... "How are things between the two of you?" as either a caring approach from someone who's concerned for the welfare of you and your spouse, or as a nosey old bag who's constantly sticking her nose into business that doesn't concern her!

Here's a short interchange I heard several years ago, again on a train...

Bill:  "I know a guy called Jake. He's not a good father. He works 18 hours a day in the city, and is obsessed with making money. He only sees his family at the weekend, what kind of supporting father is that?"

Dan:  "That's interesting, I know a Jake too, but he's not like the guy you know.  He works long hours too, but he's a great father. He cares about earning sufficient money to support his family, and uses his bonus to do fantastic things with his wife and kids; Jake Caldshaw's a great father."

Bill:  "Jake Caldshaw?"

Dan:  "Yes"

Bill:  "But... we're talking about the same guy!"

---

**Tactics:**   Be aware of, and beware of... dIstortIoN.

Sometimes it takes 'wake-up' moments, such as the above, to jolt us out of our own warped and biased thinking.

Challenge other people's assumptions of what outward behaviours actually 'mean'. Meaning is interpreted in the eye of the beholder; meaning is not the same as the outward behaviour. You will do well to separate the two in your own mind, and educate others in this respect.

---

So that's generalisation and distortion. Let's now turn our attention to the third of our thought crimes – 'deletion'.

### 3. What is 'Deletion', and why do we do it?

We delete (and critical to this is we don't even notice) information that is not relevant to us, our interests, our situation or goals.

Partly we delete information because we cannot possibly deal with the thousands of messages that we're bombarded with every day, visual, auditory, olfactory, kinaesthetic, gustatory... so we have to be selective. We also delete information that we don't want to listen to, or things that we don't want to hear – for example, when a person is giving us some 'uncomfortable' personal feedback, or when they're telling us something that doesn't fit into our personal view of the world.

In a business situation, if you interview a candidate that you immediately take a liking to, your natural human instinct is to disregard (delete) any facts or evidence that you're presented with that indicate that this person is not suitable; we talked about this in Chapter 7. If they don't have the full complement of experience that you require for example, you might disregard this fact by dismissing it as something that you can easily train them in or they can learn on-the-job. Equally, if you take an instant dislike to an interviewee it's human nature to only see the bad points, and to disregard the better qualities, even though they're staring you in the face – literally.

When we delete information we impoverish our perception of reality; it's as though we've already decided what reality is. If what we're then presented with doesn't fit, we tend to reject it as invalid. We're allowing our emotions to overrule logic and reality; effectively we're lying to ourselves, and we're lying *very* effectively.

If someone lies to you, and you don't realise they're lying, that's bad, but what can you do?

If someone lies to you, and you know they're lying you would probably expose them for lying. So you can do something about that.

If you lie to yourself, and you don't know that you are doing it, you're living a delusion.

If you lie to yourself, and you know that you are lying, you're bloody stupid!

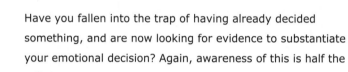

**Tactics:** Be aware of how, where and why you delete information; are you being true to yourself?

Have you fallen into the trap of having already decided something, and are now looking for evidence to substantiate your emotional decision? Again, awareness of this is half the solution.

Be conscious of how others selectively delete information that's uncomfortable for them to hear, to face up to or to bear.

Openly and publicly point out the 'forgotten' (deleted) information that others are ignoring, which you think is relevant to the discussion, and helpful to achieving the best solution.

So, the main conclusions from all the above are simply to:
- Stick to the facts
- Expose the facts when necessary
- Use the facts to your best advantage

Facts speak for themselves and are far less open to attack than opinions. They're easily defended once someone examines the data/evidence. For example, when someone announces… "This brick weighs 1.2Kg", all argument, debate and discussion are eliminated when someone else fetches a set of scales. Opinions are only that - opinions.

*"That's really nice"* may be true for you, but it's only your opinion.

I think it stinks.

# Chapter 9

## Dealing with People in the Moment

# 9
# Dealing with People in the Moment

This is where you need to be on your mettle, able to respond 'in the moment' to the day-to-day potentially frustrating actions of other people, including those who will levy criticism, or hurl abuse at you.

This subject could easily consume a whole book so I am not going to include the 90% of techniques that are obvious, and which are the usual content of books on the subject of influence and human relations. If you want to learn how to get along with, work effectively with, or just simply live alongside different types of people in a harmonious environment, then there's a lot of generic material out there already – it's good, it's just a bit bland.

Here, I am going to delve deeper, to focus upon some core principles, and then to expose some specific but less well-known psychological techniques, which again, I will illustrate using practical realistic examples to bring them to life.

Taking criticism from others, regardless of who they are, or being personally insulted, are areas that cannot be dealt with easily and there are no simple answers. However, there are things that we can do, and as before, I've peppered this chapter with a series of practical tactics. Experiment with these methods and find out what works for you. We will move from mild techniques for mild circumstances, to stronger tactics to counter more challenging situations.

## Work With Another Person's Energy, Not Against It

Fighting with people and trying to get what you want by forcing your own agenda almost always succeeds... in achieving the *opposite* of what you want! Put another way, you've failed.

I've usually found that whenever I've mentally fought with people in the past it just makes things slower, and the outcome is rarely ideal; not just for me, but also for the other person or group involved.

Why? Because the other party is pre-programmed to fight back, and if you also push back, then they're likely to escalate things still further. Why wouldn't they?

Try this experiment:

**Experiment:**    Ask someone to stand opposite you and extend both
    arms, with their palms facing you.

Now put your palms against theirs and after a second or two gently start to push their hands backwards.

I guarantee that the other person will instinctively push back in order to resist you. You did not ask them or tell them to do this; they did it purely out of human nature.

Party tricks aside, some people just can't help themselves (in both senses of the expression) from pushing back when faced with some form of resistance. In Chapter Two we discussed how people are naturally pre-programmed to behave in particular ways in order to, ultimately, ensure their survival. Unfortunately, pre-programmed, automatic short-term survival instincts don't always help us to make sensible, balanced, un-emotional decisions. They can lead to winning short-term battles, whilst compromising the longer-term campaign.

Generally speaking, the harder you push verbally or physically, the more resistance you will face. The more you push for in terms of what you want, the less you're likely to get; the harder you try, the worse you make the situation; the more desperate you are to get a boy(girl)friend, the more you repulse the really nice ones. Trying too hard. How clever is that?

In most cases there are easier ways to get what you want.

### Approach 1:  Be nice:
#### Help the other person to see what's in it for them

Often the secret lies in helping the other person to feel good about the situation or solution you propose. However, as this is a more conventional and well known approach it's not the subject of this book. Also, nice girls don't always get the guy, and vice versa. Sometime's 'nice' is over-rated; it's possible to be too nice, and we've talked about 'nice' earlier.

### Approach 2:  Be smart:
#### Outwit the other person, though without malice

In complicated cases, it's about outsmarting the other party – an intellectual game of chess, poker, or some other real-life endeavour where you need to match dishonesty with deception, treachery with trickery and manipulation with manoeuvring.

### Approach 3:  Be ruthless: Look after #1

In other situations it's about focusing upon getting your outcome rather than worrying about whether the other guy gets theirs. Now this doesn't mean that you aim for a 'you win/they lose' outcome, but rather that you focus more upon getting the outcome you require, *regardless* of the result for them. In other words their gain, loss or neutral position just doesn't figure in your calculation, because it's not significant to you; it just doesn't matter.

Now if this is beginning to sound a little selfish, please remember that in Chapter One I stated that this book is not about turning you into a 'nice guy or girl'; it's about equipping you with the tools and techniques you need to defend yourself, and to 'fare well' in an unfair world. Also, if you believe that 'nice' will always win out in the end then I wonder how you managed to read 75% of the book without tossing it onto the fire?

One of the smartest moves you can make, which has been recognised for centuries by advocates of martial arts, is to work *with*, and to *use* the energy of the other person, in martial arts terms, your adversary. Your opponent then succeeds in defeating themselves, through their own ignorance, misguided efforts and misplaced energies.

Take the example of 'road rage', something that any regular road user will have experienced at some time, if only moderately.

Imagine you're driving in the fast lane of the motorway and someone is harassing you from behind, driving too close and flashing their headlights. How do you typically react? Think about it now before you read on; how have you reacted in the past in this situation?

Here are eight possible scenarios.

1. Stay in your lane, determined that they're not going to get past you.
2. Take your foot off the accelerator, thus slowing imperceptibly and causing them to have to slow down too, and becoming progressively frustrated.

3. De-clutch and drop abruptly into a lower gear, without accelerating the engines speed to match, thus slowing your car immediately, and crucially without providing a warning brake light? Don't deny it, some of you have done this haven't you?

4. Slam your brakes on violently and watch their face in your rear view mirror as they career into the back of you [Not recommended].

5. Tickle your brake pedal, causing them to instantly react by breaking more strongly and causing them to back off - as a result of their own action.

6. Look straight ahead, feigning ignorant bliss, pretending you haven't noticed the driver behind.

7. Raise your driver's seat to its highest level, breathe in to bulk yourself up as much as you can, adopt a 'Don't mess with me' expression in the rear-view mirror, and grunt like the 'Incredible Hulk'; in order to frighten them off from daring to intimidate you.

8. Pull over into the left hand lane when safe to do so to allow them to pass.

Options 1 – 6 can be categorised as either 'aggressive' or 'passive aggressive' acts, as each is likely to end in a less than positive outcome for you. Option 7 could be described as a smart defensive move. Option 8 could be construed as weak, passive and non-assertive, until you consider how taking this option could actually be the smartest 'move' you can make… for many reasons.

By taking option 8 you move to the left lane, let the 'idiot' through, and then smartly pull back out into the fast lane directly behind them. Don't hassle the hustler in any way, but stay a safe distance behind. Now you will have a much *faster* journey to your destination as you've successfully recruited an unpaid suicidal 'lane clearer' directly ahead of you, who is pre-programmed in an unthinking automaton way to barge everyone else out of the way. It will also be a *safer* journey for you as you're driving serenely in the wake of the frazzled robotic lane clearer. You are also *less stressed* as you are able to drive with composure, un-ruffled by being harassed from behind, and your whole focus is on the road ahead... which is where it should be.

Faster, safer, less-stressed... are these not things that people would readily pay good money to experience on their next car journey?

Oh yes, you also get to watch a free 'show' as the scene continues to unfold ahead of you. Inevitably, it will contain exciting twists and turns, of both direction and plot, with new actors entering the scene from all directions. By acting in a thoughtful and intelligent manner i.e. in a 'smart' way, you get to watch the action before you without becoming part of the cast, the stressed out players or road kill. You're a dispassionate observer rather than a road rage victim.

## Head of State

Queens, Kings, Presidents, Prime Ministers, Heads of State and other important dignitaries pay tens of thousands of pounds to have the road cleared just ahead of them, in a similar manner. You can have the same service for free, if you just use your head; your own head of state.

That's what were talking about here, and throughout this book; using your head to make more intelligent choices, and to act in ways that are likely to help you rather than leave you in an unhelpful state.

Incidentally, this technique of working with another person' s energy is born out of an experience I had at age 18 when, as a newly qualified driver I was being hassled by a very aggressive driver behind me. I sped off, determined to get away from him, focusing on what was happening in my rear-view mirror. Consequently I failed to see the lady driver who had stopped in the middle of the road ahead, and who was waiting patiently to turn right. Too late; I slammed right into the back of her car, causing thousands of pounds of damage to both vehicles, hospitalising my innocent victim, and getting no end of grief thereafter from other people. It also took me several years to stop beating myself up mentally for being so stupid.

So, returning to the point, this tactic is about working *with* the energy of the other person as opposed to actively resisting them. I've alluded to martial arts and used a road rage example to illustrate the general principle, but you can use the technique in any situation where someone is using what I call 'push energy'. Your intention is to use all the energy you can muster, *including, and especially that of the other person*, in order to achieve your end objective(s).

This is not about feebly agreeing with the other person, lying down and acceding. It's about skilfully and artfully working with what you are presented with in order to intelligently do what you can, with what you have, in the circumstances in which you find yourself, right now.

Here's one more example.

Imagine a colleague or someone from another department at work comes to you to complain about the fact that you've not provided a particular service to them. If you start resisting, pushing back, defending yourself and making excuses, then how do you imagine the other person will respond? More than likely they will become even more annoyed, raise their voice, become increasingly angry, defend their position and push back even harder.

Now imagine how they would respond if you said something like...

"I'm glad you've come to see me because I've also been concerned about the situation. Clearly what we had originally agreed is not workable in practice, and it's only as we've got into the project that this has become apparent. Let's grab a coffee and work out how we can progress from here?"

In this example, it's clear the other person has an issue, and so nothing will be achieved by making excuses, arguing back, or at the other extreme, blurting cowering blithering excuses and profuse apologies.

The 'energy' that is coming from the other person needs to be received, channelled and re-directed in a direction that's going to serve your purpose, not cause you further problems. In this case you 'accept' the energy that is being directed towards you, demonstrate that you respect that there's an important issue at stake, and then 'use' the energy to push for a mutual resolution. In simple terms you're saying... "Yes, we have an issue, I agree; and you and I need to sort this out right now, so let's get our thinking caps on and find a mutually acceptable solution."

In Chapter Three we discussed how if a person wants a fight with us, then one of the most disarming tactics that you can use is to refuse to fight back, i.e. refuse to play their game. It takes two to Tango, and it also takes two to engage in a fight. It's impossible to have a verbal fight with someone who refuses to fight with you. So, here we see the application of that principle, combined with another tactic, that of proactively *using* the energy coming towards you in order to achieve a more useful and productive outcome.

Tactics

**Work with**, and therefore *use* the 'push' energy of the other person i.e. make their energy work to your advantage.

**Listen to** the other person, to quickly gain a sense of the nature of their energy, and the content of what they're saying.

**Receive** their energy and channel it in a way that they don't expect e.g. surprise them by not immediately protesting or resisting.

**Agree** with them at some level, preferably a higher level e.g. that there is an issue, or that something is not working etc.

**Re-direct** the energy, and add your own by turning the focus of the discussion towards analysis of the problem and identification of solutions, and in so doing, diffusing any personal attack.

**Retain rapport** throughout the process.

We're now going to build on the 'refusing to fight' message to link to another tactic.

## "I'm sorry, Were You Talking to Me?"

Of the other road rage options, there is another action you could consider, and from which we can derive a general principle. Option 6 was to pretend hat you hadn't noticed their overtly aggressive behaviour. Let's examine this option and see what we can learn from it in both general and specific terms.

Firstly, what do you imagine is the intention of the driver behind you who's engaged in such intimidating behaviour? What do you think they're trying to achieve by gesticulating to you from behind, crowding you by driving close or flashing their lights? In this simple case they probably just want you to get out of the way so they can push through.

However, let's broaden this random encounter to situations where, for whatever reason, someone wants to get back at you personally and wants you to feel bad in some way. If you remember one of the principles we discussed in Chapter Two, i.e. 'Nobody can make you feel anything unless you give them permission', then the same rule applies here, and it also provides a hint at a solution.

If a person wants to make someone else feel bad then they need to *know* that their tactics have been successful. After all, what they're looking to influence is not something tangible that they can objectively measure, but rather an internal emotion on both their and your part. What they want is the self-satisfaction of knowing that they have in some way 'got to you'. So, they're looking for a reaction from the other person; some sign that their 'attack' has had a psychological impact.

If they're just playing malicious mind games then they could just be seeking to get a 'rise' out of you. If, however, they get no response, or it's not the response they expect, then they're left in a state of confusion, uncertain of how to proceed. The attack is diffused, the power of the assault diminished.

Rather than achieving their intention they find themselves progressively frustrated by not getting a 'reaction' out of you. The 'ball' is still sitting on their side of the 'net'. They haven't scored the annihilating ace, or had the fun of beating you in a rally; they're the ones who find the ball dribbling back towards them from the net. They're the ones who have to pick it up and try again, but this time they won't be so confident of hitting a winner.

Bearing in mind their intention, and the fact that you want to thwart this malicious intent, then one of the simplest things you could do, certainly in the initial stages, is to not give them what they want, by ignoring them. You refuse to rise to their deliberate, coarse, un-sophisticated provocation; you don't react in the way they expect; in fact you don't react at all.

By ignoring the other person, or at least being seen not to have noticed, then the options available to the provocateur significantly narrow at this point. As what they're doing isn't working, they will be forced to either withdraw, or to do something else.

Regardless of their next course of action, you retain several options. If pushed (physically) you can push back; if attacked physically you can choose to defend yourself; and if they simply taunt your lack of courage to come back at them, then you can either discharge their immaturity with a laugh or a dismissive wave, or come back fighting at a later date. You appear to walk away from the 'battle', but you have your eye on winning the greater 'war'. Earlier I used the term 'campaign', but as we start to explore the more malicious tactics of others, it may increasingly be appropriate to use the term 'war'.

The point is that you are refusing to lower yourself to their level, something we discussed in Chapter Four, and in so doing the other person only diminishes themselves in the eyes of others.

> **Tactics:** Ignore them.
>
> Pretend you haven't noticed.
>
> Sacrifice a short term battle, for a longer-term victory.

We spoke in Chapter Seven about the power of silence, and so, far from being a weak avoidance of the issue, we're using it in this context as a proactive, conscious tactic. We're choosing to use non-reaction as a provocative tool in itself.

## Voicemail, Email, Hate Mail...

Like all tools, it won't work in every situation, and in face-to-face encounters it's certainly harder to completely ignore what another person says to you. However, one of the most effective areas in which you can use the tactic of 'ignoring' another's comments is in relation to voicemail or e-mail messages.

Often, what people say to an inanimate machine can be less thought through than what they may say face-to-face. E-mail in particular, is notorious for poorly communicated messages, and misinterpreted often negatively framed meaning.

Also, some people have a tendency to use e-mail to 'rant' about an issue, using it to 'download' their opinions or criticisms without any real-time opposition. If this is fuelled by a couple of drinks in the evening, as they furiously thumb their Blackberry keypad at the end of a stressful day, then the content can tip from assertion to plain bloody rude. In the cold light of morning, and having slept on the issue, they may regret blowing off, or is it 'thumbing off' in such a manner. By then of course, it's too late. Digital destruction is self-assured.

So, if you find yourself on the receiving end of a ranting or brusque e-mail or voicemail, you at least have the advantage of not having to react there and then. You have time to compose yourself, time to think, and time to consider how and whether you will respond. In discussing the 'Stimulus – Response' model in Chapter Two, we emphasised that one of the most important aspects of the model was the 'space' between stimulus and response, which allows you to pause and consider your reaction.

Having considered your reaction, one option open to you is to do nothing; you almost always have the 'Do nothing' option.

I have practised this technique on many occasions, especially with regards to voice mail and e-mail, and find it one of the most useful tools in my psychological kit bag. Clearly, as with any technique, if over-used then it suffers from diminishing returns and it's not possible to go through life ignoring every ranting e-mail or voicemail. The key, as with all of the tools in this book, is to intelligently use the technique when it is most appropriate to do so i.e. when it is most likely to give you the outcome you desire.

> **Tactics:** Ignore (selected) ranting e-mails and voicemails.
>
> If the sender later comes back to you to demand why you have not responded, you can always reply along the lines of... "Yes, considering the nature of the content of your e-mail (voicemail) I am still considering how best to respond to you on that."

Let's now tell people directly, just how unreasonable they can be.

## Expose People for Being 'Unreasonable'

Nobody, except the most hardened, arrogant or aggressive individual, wants to appear unreasonable. To act in an unreasonable way or to make unreasonable demands is, by definition, 'unreasonable', and hence has connotations of unfairness, childishness and a lack of professionalism. All of this boils down to unacceptable behaviour, which cannot be tolerated, and you will certainly refuse to tolerate.

The strategy here is to hold your ground and not to give in. However, rather than using unsophisticated blunt techniques such as stubbornness, arguing, raising your voice, getting emotional, digging your heels in, using your biro to stab them in the eye etc... all childish behaviours, which are open to their own accusations of being unreasonable... you adopt a 'higher' position; a higher moral ground.

Remember, none of these techniques are guaranteed to work in every situation. However, they do give you a potential advantage as they go beyond how most people deal with such situations.

You can choose to cackle and fight in the dust, and to drag yourself down to the level of the other person, or you can elect to rise above the scrapping, and encourage them to do so too. Who can argue with someone who is appealing to fair, decent, professional and reasonable behaviour? Only someone, I would suggest, who is not fair, decent, professional nor reasonable.

Occasionally you will meet such a person, for example the foul-mouthed aggressor who tells you in very clear language where to stick it, or that they spotted the taxi first and so you can just "f*** off out of it, you ******* ****!" But again, no manner of best practice technique is going to reason with someone who refuses to be reasonable, or who does not have the intellectual capability to even comprehend the meaning of the word, let alone spell it.

So, the 'unreasonableness' technique relies upon you highlighting to the other person how their actions are unreasonable in a fair world, morally reprehensible and just 'not done' within a decent society. If they are neither fair, moralistic nor decent, then it won't work, and you might get your lights punched out right there on the pavement for being such a 'pompous t***'.

An elegant way of drawing attention to a person's unreasonableness, relies upon appealing to their ego, and enabling them to save face, as in...

*"You know, I have always thought of you as a reasonable person."*

By making such a statement you are giving them an opportunity to agree with your perception of them as having always been reasonable in the past, and to continue to uphold this positive impression. Effectively you are paying them a compliment (even if not entirely true), and giving them the chance to prove you right! It then becomes more difficult for them to be unreasonable, and if they are, then they are losing something i.e. their reputation for being reasonable. Stronger ways of stating this would be...

*"You know, I had always thought that you were a reasonable person."*
(This implies that your perception is now changing)

*"In the past, I used to think of you as a reasonable person."*
(This implies that your perception has now changed)

*"In the past, I was taken in by thinking that you were reasonable"*
(Implies that you now realise that this person has never been reasonable)

**Tactics:**  Show how they are being:

- Unreasonable

- Amoral

- Unfair

- Unprofessional

In so doing, you are now continuing the discussion from a new position, and therefore controlling it

Use one or more of the statements on the previous page

What else can we do?

One of the most effective techniques is to ask the other person to 'put themselves in your shoes'. You're effectively asking them to mentally take your position for a brief period, to experience the situation through your eyes, to understand the constraints and pressures on you and to consider life from your perspective.

Remember, you're not asking them to become you; you're merely asking them to consider the situation from where you stand, and for just a few moments.

If they refuse to do this then you can 'apply the tactic to the tactic', i.e. by showing them how their refusal to consider your position is, in itself, unreasonable; they're being unreasonable in their unreasonableness. How unreasonable is that?

You can then go one step further by demonstrating how reasonable *you* are, as you're prepared to see things from their perspective. It would be a really hard-nosed person who, despite your willingness to see things from their side of the fence, was not even prepared to consider what the situation looks like from your side.

Note: Even if you demonstrate an understanding of their side of the situation, if they choose to continue to be unreasonable then you still retain the right to act in whatever way you choose. It's a case of...

*"If you're not prepared to partner with me in this, and to be reasonable, then I'm afraid all bets are off / my 'gloves' are coming off."*

Offers should always be made 'conditional', and if the other party is refusing to play fair, or to play the game at all, then they have effectively thrown away the 'rule book' and so you can change how you interpret the rules from this point forwards, if indeed there are any rules from this point forward.

Last week I checked into a long-haul flight from Abu Dhabi. On passing through passport control and security checks I realised to my horror that I had left my travel wallet on the check-in desk. Fortunatly I had my passport in my jacket pocket, but the wallet contained several important documents plus my ipod and other things I did not want to lose.

After explaining my situation to the security screener, and having a complete and absolute refusal to go back to the 'land' side, I tried other authorities such as the 'Gulf Air' customer service desk and even the airport police. All said they could not help and I had to go to the departure gate without my wallet.

My frustration was mounting as every technique I tried fell upon deaf bureaucratic ears. Finally in one last desperate attempt I went back to the security screener and literally pleaded with him using the 'put yourself in my situation' technique. "How would you feel..." I asked... "If you were in my situation? Surely, you'd want someone to help you? Please, put yourself in my shoes and understand how I am feeling right now."

He caved, and all security rules were lifted. I was escorted back out through all checkpoints and thankfully, found the check-in clerk holding onto my document wallet!

Desperate times call for desperate measures. Needless to say, I thanked him publicly and profusely, almost shaking his hand off in the process. He had made my day, and by his proud smiles and look in his eyes I'd made his. It costs nothing.

---

**Tactics:** Ask the other party to take a walk in your shoes for a while.
 Demonstrate that you're also prepared to see their side of things.

If they refuse to see your side, then explain to them how this is unreasonable of them, and not likely to lead to an amicable result for either of you.

Explain that most solutions to issues depend upon a mutual understanding of the other person's position, and that it's only fair and reasonable that both parties play their part in seeking a solution and not just highlighting problems.

---

Okay... they're still refusing to be reasonable. What now?

Stick to the facts as they do not rely upon subjective emotion.

## Stick to the Facts

Do you agree that?

- The Earth is round (ish)

- 2 + 2 = 4

- The sun will rise tomorrow

- You will die... eventually

- Latvian folk-dancing is an acquired pastime

All of the above, with the possible exception of the last statement, are true and undeniable; unless the person looking to argue is wearing one of those special white jackets with the long arms that tie around the back.

As we discussed in the previous chapter, if you want to stay on safe, neutral, and controlled ground, then there are few pieces of advice better than simply to stick to the facts. When encountering pushback you need to be on terra firma; the most concrete being the territory of incontrovertible fact. Many of the crimes highlighted in Chapter Seven are a result of someone breaking this rule, inventing their own twisted and warped view of reality, and imposing their own prejudices and value judgements upon the world. Don't fall into this trap yourself.

We also discussed in Chapter Eight the difference between perception and reality, and the problems that this can cause when two individuals interpret the same situation in contrasting ways.

So, in order to deal with this...

**Tactics:**  Stick to the facts.

Check your facts.

Challenge other people when they disguise opinion as fact.

Talk to them about the concepts of 'perception' and 'reality'.

## Keep Emotion Out Of It

Abraham Lincoln famously said… "Never write a letter when you're angry." If he were alive today I think he might have quickly added "…or fire off an e-mail."

If you're like me, then you will have broken this rule several times, and probably lived to regret it. At least, like me, you lived!

We're all emotional human beings. However, uncontrolled emotions rarely have a legitimate place in robust argument and debate, particularly within pragmatic business circles. There *is* a place for the deliberate and conscious 'tactical' use of emotion, but it's not here; see later in this chapter.

If you allow yourself to become emotional in the face of a strong adversary, or to use emotional arguments when dealing with a hard-nosed, pragmatist, then they are likely to view this as a sign of weakness, which they will then use against you.

Put yourself in the 'receiving' position for a moment. How do you feel about, and react towards, people who become emotional? Do you have sympathy for them; in which case you may regard them as being in a weak, disempowered position? This is just one interpretation, but you will note that within the word 'sympathetic' lies the word 'pathetic'. In this state they're hardly portraying themselves as being in full control of the situation. They may come across as helpless, hapless and hopeless, and in the extreme could be signalling desperation.

Alternatively, do you think 'Pull yourself together you wimp'?

Either way, the person who allows themselves to become emotional is demonstrating a position of weakness, subservience or at least of not being in full control of themselves or the situation. Note, I said 'allows' themselves to become emotional, as there's an important distinction between being a victim of emotion and in *using* emotion in a conscious and planned manner. In the former case you're an emotional wreck, in the latter you're being an 'emotional tactician'.

The point is that if you allow yourself to become emotional then you are far less likely to be able to assert a strong influence upon the situation.

Think about the last time you witnessed a person getting angry. Maybe you're thinking of times when you've become angry? How in control do you think this person is when they're right there in the thick of the emotion? Not very, I would suggest. Others may remark afterwards… "He completely lost control"… "She went off at the deep end", or other expressions indicating a highly emotionally charged, uncontrolled reaction.

So, the simple message from this section is that if you want to retain the maximum control and influence over a situation then keep emotions out of it.

> **Tactics:** Never write a letter or fire off an e-mail when you're angry.
>
>
>
> When you allow yourself to become emotional, you lose a degree of personal composure and of control of the situation and outcome, so, keep 'unplanned' and 'uncontrolled' emotions out of your influencing toolkit.

## 'Help Me to Help You' Technique

Most people will have great difficulty in not responding positively to this smart technique. This is because you're asking them to 'help you to help them', something which is clearly in their interest. Essentially you're saying… "Put me in a position in which I can assist you in the best way I can, so that you get what you want."

Imagine you're in a shop, trying to return some high-value product that you bought the previous day, but for which you do not have a receipt. Clearly there is some doubt as to whether you bought the goods from this particular outlet. The assistant says 'I want to be able to give you your money back, but in order for me to do that, I need you to fill in this short form.' Would you fill in a four or five line form in order to get your money back? After all, she's only asking you to help her to give you what you want – your money back. Of course you would. You'd especially fill in the form if you'd nicked the item from the shop in the first place!

This is a simple illustration of the 'Help me to help you' technique in action. A technique that you can apply in situations far more significant than just getting £39:99 back for a chocolate fountain… that you only realised you didn't want once you'd got it home.

Have you ever worked for a control freak, or know someone who has? Imagine you've got a boss that is overly controlling. They're constantly on your back, checking what you do, giving you direction and advice. You feel as though you're being continually checked-up on, and having your activities and work-quality scrutinised. Their behaviour is really not helping you to perform at your best; in fact, it's slowing you down and making you lose confidence in your ability.

Here's a classic example of where you can practically use the 'Help me to help you' technique... on your boss.

> *"Steve, I know that getting these projects finished on time is critical to you, and you're keen to ensure that the work that goes out from our department is of a high standard. I feel exactly the same way."*

> > *NB: At this early stage in the dialogue can you identify which technique, that we've already discussed, the speaker is using?*

> *"Steve, in fact, because I do a lot of the ground work, and put in the details, I am doubly sensitive to ensuring that the data and figures are accurate and current. However, I get the feeling that you don't trust me to do my job, because it seems as though you're constantly hovering over my workstation and checking up on me. That makes me doubly cautious, which means that I'm taking twice as long as normal to get the information to you; I'm triple-checking stuff that doesn't even need double-checking. This is not only wasting my time, and therefore the company's time and money, it also means that we get stuff out to the customers later than we could.*

*Steve, I need your help on this one. I need you to 'help me to help you', because the way that you're managing me right now is not getting the very best out of me."*

This is a long example, though one that hopefully makes the point. Could you imagine using such a technique yourself if you found yourself in the situation above?

I hope so, because not only is it assertive, it's also proactive, respective of the other person, and aimed at achieving mutual benefits for the company, their manager and themselves.

It's difficult to imagine how any right-thinking manager could object to such a proposal.

---

**Tactic:**   Use the 'Help Me to Help You' technique

---

## 'Natural Consequences' Technique

As you will have discovered throughout this book, some of the most powerful techniques are elegantly simple, and this is no exception.

Have you ever heard yourself say something like... "You know, I just knew that was going to happen / they would react that way / she would dig her heels in over this / they would go behind my back / he'd walk out on me"... etc?

Alternatively, how many times have you thought, or even said "I told you so" to a friend, who had acted against your advice?

As intelligent beings we can pretty much guess how things might pan out over time, even though life and people insist on throwing us occasional curve balls. The 'natural consequences' technique taps into this innate human capability of prediction by directing the discussion down the path of most likely outcome.

Simply put, it involves nothing more than asking the other person what they think is likely to happen if they continue to act in the way that they've been operating so far, or if they take the action that they are contemplating or threatening?

Note, you don't *tell* the other person what the natural consequences are, you *ask* them, and in so doing you leverage the power of questions. This is a very important distinction, so ensure you get it the right way around.

In a 'let me tell you' world, questions are under-rated as tools of influence, yet they are *the* tools of the master influencer, and are one of the main reasons behind the success of the world's best hypnotists and sales people.

Which do you think is likely to be the more powerful technique in influencing people?

1. Asking people questions and allowing them to answer, even if only non-verbally within the confines of their own mind

2. Making statements, telling them something or telling them how to think

If you chose (1) then, not only did you get it right, in doing so you also proved the validity of the technique as it was *you* who told *yourself* what to believe. All I did was to as you the question. I influenced you and I don't even know you.

Here are some simple questions that you can use to explore natural consequences with a person whom you wish to influence.

You: *"Bill, what do you think is likely to happen if we continue in this way?"*

You: *"Angie, if you were in my position, how would you react to what you are asking of me?"*

You: *"Nazmi, I can't stop you. I can only advise you at this point. But have you thought about how the senior team might react if you persist in implementing this idea? Do you really think you will get the support you imagine?"*

This is a bit like saying "if you pull the plug out of the sink what do you think might happen to the water?" or "If you carry on contradicting and humiliating your boss in public, what hope can you legitimately hold for that promotion?"

Asking the other person to imagine the natural consequences of their current course of action is a powerful technique for personal change because you're forcing them to paint a picture in their own mind of the future. That future maybe doesn't look quite so pleasant once they think it through logically and play the 'video tape' of the future in their mind's eye.

As an aside, whilst I was writing the above paragraph, I found myself wondering what colour the worktops are in your kitchen.

No, I haven't gone mad or wildly off track. However, I am pretty confident that it was not possible for you to read on without instantly answering the kitchen worktop question in your own mind. Recall, we talked about this in Chapter 5. You see, in order to *understand* the question your mind will automatically throw out answers – whether you want it to or not.

Are they granite, pine, white melamine...?

Who cares, and don't bother to write in, I'm not really interested in your kitchen worktops. What I *am* interested in is how people can control the minds of others without them even being aware of it, let alone being able to stop them.

### *Your mind is smarter than you think*

Think about that statement for a moment, and consider who exactly is in charge of your thinking? Are you in charge of your mind, or is your mind in charge of you? Who minds your mind? Who's doing the thinking about your thinking? Do you have another brain to do that bit or does your brain think about and moderate itself? How would it know it was right?

Imagine if someone were to ask you how guilty you were feeling about letting them down in the meeting yesterday? Now in order to answer the question, your mind has to do several things in very quick succession:

1. You have to understand and bring to the forefront of your mind what is meant by the word 'guilt', and any emotions attached to it

2. You run a super-fast 'video tape' in your head of the meeting you attended yesterday, or at least recall a still image representing the scene

3. Finally, you attempt to connect 1 and 2 so that you can identify what it was that you did, or did not do that you should be feeling guilty about?

All of the above happens in a fraction of a second, and only then are you able to respond in a meaningful way.

You're also very unlikely to be thinking about your thinking.

Your response could of course be to protest that you did no such thing, and that you do not feel the slightest sense of guilt. Unfortunately, by then it's too late, the malicious seed has already taken root. My point is that the questioner has influenced your mind instantaneously without *telling* you how to feel, but rather by asking you about a feeling. They achieved this through the clever use of a manipulative, leading question, 'How guilty do you feel?'

The question is not '*Are* you feeling guilty?' but about the *degree* to which you feel guilt; the guilt is taken as a given, it is pre-supposed, the pernicious question is simply about degree. Effectively the questioner has slipped in the guilt trip via the Trojan Horse of a tangential question.

Here's a light hearted way of looking at how these malicious suppositions can be established through simple conversation and questioning:

Gent:      *"Madam, will you sleep with me for £5?"*

Woman:   "Certainly not – how dare you!"

Gent:      *"Well would you sleep with me for £5,000?"*

Woman:   [Hesitatingly] ... "Possibly"

Gent:      *"What about £50?"*

Woman:   "Look, what do you take me for; a common prostitute!?"

Gent:      *"Madam, we have already established what you are; all we're doing now is haggling over the price."*

---

> **Tactics:** Use the 'Natural Consequences' technique.
>
>  Practice planting seeds in other people's minds using the
> questioning technique illustrated above; for example:
>
> - "How excited are you going to feel when...?"
>
> - "Are you going to be angry or relieved when...?"
>
> - "Just before you leave..."
>
> - "Aren't you worried that...?"
>
> Raise your conscious awareness of where and when others
> use this technique on you.
>
> NB, most people aren't clever enough to use this consciously,
> and in which case they let slip an unconscious clue as to how
> *they* are viewing a situation.

---

In answer to the last point, if a person says something like "Aren't you worried that...?" or "Don't you fear that someone will take advantage of you when...?" it probably says more about their state of mind, and indicates that *they're* likely to take advantage of a person, rather than an indicator of your own state of mental health. With their cautious, suspicious question they reveal the deeper suspicions of their own mind.

## Use Emotion

*"Hey!"...* I hear you say... *"You just said not to get emotional!"*

Yes I did, and I stand by that rule.

Let me be very, very clear. What we are talking about here is the deliberate and conscious tactical *use* of emotion. The distinction is that you're *using*

emotion; you are not allowing emotion to take control of you i.e. you are not *getting* emotional. As I emphasised earlier, there's a huge difference between the two situations.

So, we are not, under any circumstances, talking about you becoming emotional; that would go against the whole tenet of this book. There is a world of difference between...

1. Telling someone in an assertive way how their behaviour is affecting you

   and

2. Becoming irate, frustrated, angry or breaking down in tears in front of them

The former is an assertive, highly controlled and conscious ploy, intended to influence the other person by, for example, helping them to see how unreasonable they're being ('Unreasonable Behaviour' technique), or by pointing out the consequences of them continuing to behave in this way ('Natural Consequences' technique).

Compare the two responses below:

1. "Gary, I need to tell you how I am feeling about this situation. I think the time has come to lift ourselves out of the detail and discuss what's going on at broader level. It's clear to me that we're not making the progress that I, and I'm sure you, would like. I feel that your lack of willingness to provide the level of resources we need for this project puts us all in an untenable position, and is jeopardising the whole endeavour. Consequently I'm feeling frustrated, and right now I can't see us resolving this unless you're prepared to be flexible on the resourcing issue."

2. "Gary I've had it, I really have. I'm at my wits end [looks away]. I've tried to explain to you a million times that we desperately need more manpower

and budget for this project [throws hands in the air]. I'm feeling in a hopeless and powerless situation and I don't think you appreciate how stressed out about this I am right now. I've been working all hours just to keep this thing together, [puts head in hands] I'm pissed off, fed up and I don't think you give a shit!" [starts to well up with tears].

Even though you're only reading the words off the page, and cannot see the accompanying non-verbal gestures and facial expressions of both speakers, nor the intonation, the difference between the two approaches will be starkly apparent. More importantly, their outcomes will be worlds apart.

In the first example the speaker is consciously using an emotional argument in order to influence; and is doing so in a professional, assertive and controlled manner. The second person however, has allowed themselves to become emotional, and displayed a very weak, almost pathetic position as a consequence.

I don't need to ask which response is likely to yield the most useful outcome… but then by telling you what I don't need to ask , you've already asked and answered the question I didn't ask you in your own mind!

---

**Tactics:** Use emotional argument in a conscious, deliberate fashion, as an additional tool that you choose to select from your kit bag.

Never allow emotion to get the better of you.

---

## Use the 'Time Machine'

Time, we're told, is a great healer. Time certainly helps to heal physical wounds and scars, and many would agree that the passage of time also facilitates the healing of emotional scars, and in diminishing their associated feelings. We referred to this in Chapter Five when we discussed the importance of getting things into their proper context, time frame and perspective.

However, 'time' means different things to different people. To some it means 'money' (as in the expression, 'time is money), to others it's a 'pressure cooker' ('I've only got an hour to get this bloody report out'), an 'enemy' (from the prisoner's perspective), or a 'friend' to Louis Armstrong (as in, "We've got all the time in the world").

So, because it can mean different, even polarised, yet very important things to different people, the key is to recognise the importance and significance of time to both you and the other party, and how this might differ; and then to use the 'Time Machine' in an intelligent and appropriate manner.

For example, in a negotiation situation it's well known that the person who has, or perceives themselves to have less time than the other party, will feel a disproportionate amount of pressure to reach a conclusion. As a consequence, they're far more likely to concede their position prematurely, and to give too much away too soon. So, as a canny negotiator, if you have more time, or can *create the impression* that you're in no hurry to reach a conclusion, then this can have a powerful effect upon the other party – significantly to your advantage.

Is this manipulation? Yes

Should you be bothered ('bovvered')? Only if it's being used against you

Why?

Because it's a legitimate, and well-used negotiation tactic that others have used against you on previous occasions. Perhaps it's only now, when you think back over such situations, that you realise this. As such, you should be as aware and as equipped as anyone to use it when required.

In more than 15 years working as both a negotiator and in training others to negotiate, I have found that the time pressure to reach a deal, often more than any other factor, including money, is hugely important in determining the outcome of a negotiation.

So, how can you take control of the 'Time Machine' and use it to your advantage? Let's talk about two similar, but different techniques; 'strategic withdrawal' and 'postponement', remembering in every case, that these are conscious acts rather than 'running away' behaviours.

## 1. Strategic withdrawal

Strategic withdrawal, or deliberately taking a break, is definitely not a 'running away' behaviour because it does exactly what it says on the 'tin', i.e. it's a conscious and deliberate strategic withdrawal on your part to temporarily extract yourself from the situation. The key to strategic withdrawal is that you only remove yourself *temporarily*, with a clear, communicated intention to re-engage in the near future.

There are many benefits to using this tactic in everyday social and business interactions including:

- Buying you thinking time.

- Enabling you to do more research.

- Giving you time to consult other people, ask their opinion and seek ideas for alternative courses of action.

- Putting you in the 'driving seat' so you dictate the pace of events.

- Potentially un-nerving the other party as they wonder what you're up to, (even if you *are* only buying time, they cannot know for sure).

- Enabling events to unfold around you, which can often change the dynamics of the situation. "Let's cross that bridge when we come to it" is often a sensible strategy because as time moves on you gain access to more accurate information, which means you're more likely to make good decisions.

Sometimes a rush to action is premature, and as events unfold with the passage of time you find that you engaged in unnecessary work.

A former boss approached me some years ago, wanting a quick decision on a Friday about the re-structuring of my department. The discussion felt rushed and there was a lot to think about. I chose to use strategic withdrawal for no other reason than I needed to buy myself some time to think through the situation. I said I would need to think about it over the weekend, and would come back to him on Monday with my considered thoughts; not an unreasonable request.

Note how this is an example of using two techniques together:

1. Appealing to 'reasonable' behaviour i.e. for the other person not to be unreasonable, and to respect your reasonable requests, and

2. Using your 'Time Machine'.

When I returned on Monday I presented a counter-proposal. I was able to do this because I had bought myself sufficient thinking time to weigh up the pros and the cons, and to consider alternative scenarios. It had also given me time to speak to a few friends over the weekend, to ask their advice over a few drinks, and to seek their ideas about alternative solutions. I asked them what they would do if faced with this situation.

I won't bore you with the counter-proposal, other than to say that after a short discussion it was accepted by my boss as a more sensible and workable way forward. The fact that I saved two people's jobs made this technique worth its weight in gold, and justifies the time I've invested in writing this book. By the way, if you were one of those two people you'll never know what you never knew.

> **Tactic:**  Use 'Strategic Withdrawal' when you want to buy yourself some time or to take advantage of any of the other benefits identified above.

Preserving livelihoods and careers aside, how else can we use the 'Time Machine'?

## 2. Postponement

Are we splitting hairs here? I can hear some readers asking... "What's the difference between postponement and withdrawal?" I could make a tasteless joke at this point, but I won't; I'll simply let your mind do it for you.

For me a postponement, in the business sense, is worse than delay; postponement signals cancellation, and to me, that's terminal.

Believe me, as a trainer, speaker and facilitator of similar events, a 'postponement' is more often than not a euphemism for cancellation. Beware if anyone tells you that they're postponing an action, or a decision about something to a later date. Postponement doesn't always mean postponement;

it's a bit like "The cheque's in the post", it fundamentally creates uncertainty about whether what has been previously agreed will ever happen at all.

I believe the reason for this is that most people don't like reneging on deals, saying "No", or simply having to give bad news to others. It's far easier to say we're postponing a decision (even though they know it's a 'No'), than saying "No" directly to someone, here and now.

What can perpetuate this is when the other person doesn't like hearing "No" and would prefer to choose to interpret postponement or delay as just that, even if deep down they suspect rejection. It's a face-saving manoeuvre in which they knowingly deceive themselves. We talked about the dangers of lying to yourself in Chapter eight.

So how can an appreciation of this typical human behaviour help you?

Firstly, if you're the one who's announcing a postponement then you can use this to your advantage, as you simply refer to the postponement as what it is… a postponement. Even though you've probably already decided not to go ahead, the other party cannot know this, even if they suspect it, and so it buys you time. It buys you a 'Get Out Of Jail Free' card which means that you can either re-book and re-engage, or give the 'postponed' bad news at a later date.

| | |
|---|---|
| Cowardly? | Yes |
| Ethical? | No |
| Common practice? | Yes |

When it's 'dog eat dog' you have to play the buggers at their own game. I'm not suggesting you use this tactic as part of your daily method of interacting with people who are important to you, or that you care about. In business and life in general, if you do this too often then you lose the trust of others. I'm simply suggesting that for some people, and in some circumstances, you may wish to play people at their own 'game'.

So, what about people who postpone on you?

Because it's difficult to expose, this is tricky, and it depends largely upon the power balance between you and the other party. Personally, given the experience I've had over the years, I would treat any postponement in the way I'm describing above i.e. I would regard it as a cancellation in disguise.

Your responses may include…

"Steve, I appreciate that you now need to put our original dates back, but clearly I cannot confirm or guarantee dates for the future unless you're able to give me a firm booking in writing."

"Greg, I really hate to have to refer to this, but as you know, we have a cancellation policy. As you're not able to give us much notice, it's highly unlikely that we'll be able to re-allocate those dates to other clients. Is there anything we can do to stick to the original dates in order to prevent us having to levy a cancellation charge?"

"Jenny, is this really a postponement, or is it just a gentle way of letting me down? I would much rather that we were totally clear about the situation, and if you've no intention of going ahead then I'd really much prefer it if you told me so now, so that I can make alternative plans."

This latter example is an interesting one as some people may regard it as a bit of a risk. Why? Because, as I mentioned earlier, they may then just hear what it is that they don't want to hear i.e. "If I don't push for a decision then I can't be rejected."

I would add one word to that statement, which is… "yet".

Isn't it better, if you're going to be let down, that you know about it now rather than hanging onto some lame hope for the future, which in all likelihood is not going to be realised? Doesn't knowing about it up front at least give you information that will enable you to consider what other POCA's you have available? If you've forgotten about your POCA's then refer back to Chapter Five.

We often hear that 'Information is Power', and I stated earlier that the person with the most options has the most flexibility, and hence the most control over a situation. If you're allowing yourself to be deluded then you're operating from a point of misinformation, and therefore from a disadvantaged position. Remember, if you're lying to yourself, and you know that you're lying, you're bloody stupid. So, grit your teeth and flush out the reality of the situation in order to then move on to a more informed, and therefore potentially more powerful position.

**Tactics**

Use 'postponement' whenever you want to cancel, but either can't bring yourself to give the bad news, or when you want to keep the other person dangling on a string... a string that you will eventually cut.

Warning: Don't use this tactic with people who are important to you or with whom you want to build longer-term trusting relationships.

If another person tells you that a decision has been postponed, then treat it as a cancellation, more often than not that's what it is.

Flush out postponements to find out if they are simply euphemisms for cancellation.

Move on and focus on people who are able to give you firmer commitments. To do otherwise, is to regale yourself to a weaker, overly dependent position, and one that is potentially very time-consuming and frustrating. Remember however, it all depends upon the power balance between you and the other party.

## Dealing with 'Telesales Callers'

Telesales person:    *"Good afternoon Mr.Lavelle, I'm doing a survey on replacement doors and windows and wondered if you have a couple of minutes to answer a few questions?"*

Me:    "Oh I'm so glad you called because I'd like to talk to you about Jesus; do you know that he died to save our souls?"

Try it; I did, and it worked immediately, as the young woman on the end of the telephone didn't know how to respond, other than to apologise in a confused and flustered way, and to quickly hang up.

But the story doesn't end there, as 10 minutes later the phone rang again. This time it was a man, I assume a colleague of the telesales woman, who announced himself by saying… "Good afternoon Mr.Lavelle… this is the Devil!"

So, when you play with fire, you also need to be prepared for instances where people play you at your own game, in this case with no less than the Devil's fire himself!

The point about this true story, is that when people get so focused on saying what it is that they want to say, and in taking you down a track that has been pre-engineered, you can use the fact that they are on a monorail to quickly and effectively de-rail them.

If they, like you, had a range of POCA's, then they would be in an empowered position to be able to quickly and effectively change tack (track), and still retain an element of control. In fact your opinion of them may ascend instantly. Unfortunately, as we know all too well, the numbskulls employed by most telesales agencies are not operating as thinking human beings, but as automatons who are taught or deliberately constrained by just one approach. Once you try to engage them in a conversation that is not 'part of the script', they're completely floored, and unable to respond in any intelligent or helpful manner.

I've played like this on numerous occasions with people who try to sell things to me, and I encourage you to do the same, purely as an education and learning experience. If, in the process, you derive some form of self-satisfied pleasure from toying with people like this, or even a worthwhile discount, then that's a bonus. However, my recommendation is to use the fact that they've telephoned you in their own time, and at their own expense, to derive some developmental benefit from the conversation yourself.

This is not the place to list a whole series of specific verbal techniques for dealing with such 'narrow' instances, as each situation will be different. My main point is for you to use each telesales imposition as a harmless and inconsequential practice ground for your development. Most people hate being called by telephone sales people, so why not change how you frame the situation and use it to your advantage? It's another example of the provocative tactic of doing the opposite of what other people expect, a technique we explored in Chapter Five.

So, this is not an exhaustive list of reposts, however for illustration, I've included here a few responses that I recall using in the past.

Caller 1:  *"Are you considering taking a holiday within the next year?"*

Me:  "No, I don't like holidays, I much prefer to work."

... or

"No, you see I'm agoraphobic – I can't go out of the house."

... or

"No, I can't; you see I'm an albino, and I react violently when I am exposed to daylight, or I find that other people attack me, something to do with an anarchic myth about wanting to boil up my legs to make a medicine."

... or

"It's going to be difficult, as it looks like I might be facing a jail sentence within the next few weeks."

| | |
|---|---|
| Caller 2: | *"Do you have a minute to answer a few market research questions about XYZ?"* |
| Me: | "If you really mean 'a minute' then okay, however, I will be putting the telephone down after exactly 60 seconds." |
| | |
| Caller 3: | *"If I could save you more than £200 off your annual gas bill would you be interested?"* |
| Me: | "No." |
| Caller 3: | *"Really? Why not?"* |
| Me: | "Because I am extremely rich, and so £200 to me is not even worth thinking about. Are you rich? I am; it's brilliant!" |

... or

| | |
|---|---|
| Me: | "Not really. There are more significant things I need to sort out right now; such as how to re-gain custody of my children, repairing a damaged relationship with my father's boyfriend, and coming to terms with losing my job. Can you help me with any of these things?" |

Caller 4: *"I'm calling you about XYZ, which is selling so fast we didn't want you to miss out on your chance of buying one before they all run out."*

Me: "Well, if you're selling them so fast, why do you need to call people like me? It sounds as though you will sell them all by the end of the day without any effort whatsoever on your part. Good luck!" [Hang up].

Caller 5: *"I'm giving you a quick call to ask you about ABC."*

Me: "I'm sorry… I think the police are at the door." [Hang up].

Caller 6: *"Do you have a moment to answer a few market research questions about XYZ?"*

Me: [Sighing]. "Thank you so much for calling. Do you know what I find really depressing? The fact that no-one seems to call me anymore, apart from nice people like you, who really *do* seem to care about me and want to talk. Most people seem to have drifted away from me over the years, and now I hardly ever get the chance to talk with people on the phone; people seem just so busy to listen to me. Do you have an hour or so free right now?"

[Whatever you do, do not allow them to direct the conversation in any way, just keep bringing it back to *you* and what *you* want to talk about.]

I could go on, and so could you, much to the frustration of our piece-time caller! So if you want a bit of fun, why not have a go at sketching out some 'track de-railing' responses to the following:

Caller 7:    *"Our salesperson will be in your area next Wednesday, would it be okay for him to call round in the morning, or would the afternoon be more convenient?"*

Caller 8:    *"You've been specially selected by our computer to receive an exclusive offer that's not available to the general public."*

Caller 9:    *"Our normal price is £X, but for a limited time we're offering you the opportunity to buy one for just £Y, if you sign up today."*

How did you get on? Did you dream up some ace responses? If so, please email me at <u>jon@blueiceconsulting.co.uk</u> and I may include them in the next edition.

Here's a final technique that I have successfully employed on several occasions. The joy of this technique is that you play them at their own game i.e. the 'time-wasting' game.

Caller 10:    *"I'm phoning from Bright Glaze double glazing and conservatories."*

Me:          "Oh yes, I'm delighted you called, because we're considering building a new conservatory at the moment. You couldn't have timed your call more perfectly! Can you just give me a few seconds whilst I turn the cooker down?"

Of course, they will be more than happy to hang on the line for a few moments whilst you deal with your domestic situation. They probably won't still be there two minutes later though, when you have not returned to the phone, and have simply left the receiver off the hook! They're the ones incurring the phone call, so let them pay the bill. More importantly, someone is paying them to make X calls per hour, so their attention span is likely to be less than yours, especially as you're making valuable use of the time in attending to more important matters. How dare they disturb you at home in your own time? Make them pay with money and time of their own.

But... there's a snag. What if they call back?

Well, if they believe that you really are considering a conservatory and, for whatever reason you simply forgot to return to the telephone, or were cut off unexpectedly, they will definitely call again, after all, you're probably the only positive answer they've had all day!

If so, you need to be ready with your second response, which could include things such as:

"Oh yes, I'm sorry about that, I got distracted. It was about conservatories wasn't it. Yes, I do want to speak with you; let me just grab a pen and paper."

Once again, you don't return.

If they call a third time, then you simply deny all knowledge, saying that you think they've got the wrong number, or say something like...

"Oh I know what's happened. You were probably speaking to my twin sister/brother, who's living with us at the moment. (S)he's having professional care and isn't always in touch with reality. I'm sorry if (s)he's wasted your time. A conservatory? Oh no, I'm sorry, I think (s)he was probably talking about Christianity."

And if they still then try to hook you with the idea of a conservatory you can always respond with the guaranteed conversation stopper in relation to home improvements...

"I'm afraid there's no point in discussing that with you as we've agreed the sale of our house and will be moving in a few weeks. I really would hate to waste your time any further; thank you and goodbye!"

## Break Patterns with Humour

If you can make things funny, you can make changes, shatter destructive thinking patterns and alter emotional states... instantly.

In Chapter Seven I referred to the use of humour to deflect criticism. Humour is a great diffuser of tension, and can be used to calm difficult situations with other people. We will return to this subject again in Chapter Nine, as there are additional, personal psychological benefits to be derived from the use of humour.

Have you noticed how people without a sense of humour tend to be inflexible? I believe there's a link between the two, as inflexible, more narrow-minded people tend not to be mentally wired in a way that responds well to, feeds off or creates humour. In the work I have carried out around creativity and innovation I have also developed the belief that humour and creativity are strongly correlated. Some of the most creative individuals I have met seem to be wired in a particular way that enables them to make esoteric, often bizarre leaps of thinking.

We discussed in Chapter Seven the way in which humour works i.e. by taking us down one mental path and then jolting us out of it, often violently, to create an unexpected connection. The 'surprise' ending to an otherwise predictable sequence of events is this mental jolt that causes us to laugh. I referred in Chapter Eight to the HSBC advertisements and the phenomenon of 'neurological shock. This is not exactly the same as humour, but it is equally as powerful in jolting us out of our 'stinking thinking'.

I have just been reading Derren Brown's book 'Tricks of the Mind', and in the very first sentence is an example of the mental jolt that humour provides:

> *'Derren was born in 1971 in Croydon.*
> *It was a difficult birth – his mother was in Devon at the time.'*

I could have chosen any one of millions of jokes to illustrate the same principle. I chose this one for no other reason than I read it this morning and it made me laugh out loud.

In any machine, the part that is the most inflexible is likely to break first, particularly when the machine's put under pressure. When you're dealing with people in difficult circumstances it's likely that one or both parties are under some degree of pressure, stress or duress. Hence, humour can be an effective ice-breaker, allowing people to laugh, to immediately change state, to relax a little and to breathe.

Imagine constantly putting the wrong key in your front door when you return home. You keep getting it wrong, cursing yourself and probably damaging the lock in the process, until the day you laugh it off. After you've had a good old laugh about how absurd it is that you're getting yourself worked up into such a state over such a trivial matter, your perspective on the situation will have changed forever. You're also in a far more receptive state to think about solutions to the problem, such as colour-coding your keys, leaving the door permanently unlocked or never going out of the house. Hey, I didn't say they had to be practical solutions.

Think of times when you've found yourself in a tense situation with another person or group. Things are edgy, awkward, frosty, guarded or whatever, but as soon as someone cracks a joke, or even makes a mildly amusing remark, observation or aside, no matter how lame, it provides an intensely welcome, if only momentary, release. Everyone laughs, and relaxes just a little. The break is what was needed, a chance to release some of the pent-up pressure.

I was checking in for another flight last week in the Middle East and there was some problem with the reservation. A supervisor had to be called and a different sort of ticket was issued, during which I joked... "So, it looks like you've upgraded me to Business Class!" [I know he hadn't upgraded me, but I thought I'd make light of the situation and who knows, maybe my cheek would mean that he did].

"Well, it's '*like*' Business Class", said the clerk.

I still found myself in Economy.

'Like' Business Class... I thought this was so funny that the quip stayed with me all week and my colleagues and myself applied the crazy thinking to so many comparisons for days to come as in...

*"Do you have any orange Juice?"*
"Well, it's like orange juice."

Even in my hotel room I noticed the label on the milk cartons said 'Tastes like milk."

And a classic that happened after a meeting the next day...

*"In the negotiation did you both end up compromising?"*

"Yes. Well, It was 'like' a compromise, but on his terms."

I was once in a tense team negotiation scenario with a key client. Both sides were dancing around the issues and we were now up against a potential deal-breaking impasse. Tension had been rising in the room for 20 minutes or so, and everyone seemed to be under pressure, we were getting nowhere. Nowhere, that is, until the pressure got to one of my colleagues in such a way that he let out an involuntary 'bottom burp'! Now, that was hardly professional behaviour, and you can imagine the embarrassment that would likely ensue, potentially resulting in an abrupt end to all negotiations. No. Instead, there were a few sideways glances, a smirk or two, and before we knew it the whole room was in uproarious laughter.

I promise you this is true. Even my embarrassed colleague who had launched the air biscuit was laughing along, and was enormously relieved, literally as well as metaphorically. His unintended interjection 'said' what everyone was feeling but no-one was talking about i.e. "it's getting a bit tense in here isn't it?"

Did we close the deal? Yes, and whilst I cannot put it all down to an involuntary little fart, to this day I believe that at that moment the whole atmosphere in the room changed... in both senses of the word. Suddenly, life didn't seem so serious and the deal that we were all buttock-clenchingly holding out for was put into a new, more human perspective.

So, what can we take from this?

> **Tactics:** Use appropriate humour to break the atmosphere in tense or otherwise difficult situations.
>
> Be prepared for it to backfire, but be ready to take the risk, because if what you're doing isn't working then it's worth trying something else, and humour is as good a medicine as any; and it doesn't come with a prescription charge.
>
> Look for the humorous side of life in the everyday situations you find yourself in.

## Handling Direct Criticism

One of the most difficult situations we face is in handling criticism from others, particularly direct, open criticism. The good news is that most of us face this only rarely.

A major complication is that, as sensitive human beings, our first reaction is to react emotionally to what we're being presented with. This can then mean that we don't truly listen to what we are being told as our first instinct is to defend ourselves. If, however, when on the receiving end of negative feedback, we had a way of handling those initial feelings, then we could learn to respond more constructively. The key here is to learn how to turn criticism into feedback.

The technique I describe here has been derived from observing people who are very good at disassociating themselves from the criticism, thus removing a large chunk of emotion, and enabling them to make more thoughtful responses as a result. It's a rare skill because few people even know that this technique exists, let alone how to do it. You will either find that this is relatively easy to do, or you will twist yourself up in mental knots as you struggle to get your head around the technique.

Persist, and follow the steps below, because when you master this technique it will give you an immense advantage when dealing with criticism, and difficult situations in general.

## Disassociation Technique

**Step 1 of 5:** As you are receiving the criticism (feedback), try to disassociate yourself from the situation by becoming aware of how you are reacting. The way to do this is to imagine that you are outside of your body, watching yourself receiving the criticism. In your mind's eye you need to 'see yourself at a distance'.

Now, even as I am writing this, I imagine that you may not know what the hell I'm talking about, and as a consequence, you will just read through the other steps without really experiencing the power of this technique. You have to work with me on this and actually give the exercises a go.

So, try it now.

Try to see yourself as though you're looking at yourself in the room you're now in. Really do it, mentally picture yourself as though you are looking at yourself from the other side of the room.

Some people achieve this by firstly seeing themselves close up, and then gradually pulling back so they're eventually seeing themselves from 15 or 20 feet away, or in some cases more than 100 feet. If you can do this right now then great. If not, keep trying until you get to experience this virtual 'out-of-body' experience.

**Step 2 of 5:** When you are next in a situation where you are receiving criticism, imagine that you are creating a movie about the content of the criticism. From your new, more distant perspective, see yourself questioning the criticiser to gather as much information and clarification about the situation as possible. As we discovered in Chapter Seven, criticisms often come in vague forms such as "You're disrespectful" or "You embarrassed me." See yourself asking questions that seek information about how *specifically* you were perceived as disrespectful or embarrassing.

**Step 3 of 5:** Evaluate the criticism, objectively. Now that you have gathered

more information and clarified the situation, decide which parts you agree with, and which parts you do not. You do this by comparing the perception of the other person with the events as you recall them. If your version of events differs from theirs then gather more information and seek further clarification by questioning them.

**Step 4 of 5:** Decide upon your response. You now have virtually all the information you need in order to respond. Your response will firstly include the things that you agree with, followed by those that you don't. By doing it this way around, which is highly unusual, then you are much more likely to retain rapport with the person. Most people when faced with criticism will react emotionally, and rather than agree, will immediately lash back at the accuser, telling them just how wrong they are. Not the best starting point.

**Step 5 of 5:** Finally, make changes to your future behaviour that indicate that you have truly learned from the feedback. Not only will the other person see you as a mature and reasonable person, through your unusual reaction to criticism and subsequent actions, you will also grow and develop in terms of psychological maturity and the range of POCA's (Possibilities, Options, Choices and Alternatives) open to you.

Now... this is where you may need to fasten your mental seatbelt, because here's a challenge for only the most intelligent and capable readers.

Can you go further and watch yourself disassociate i.e. disassociate from yourself disassociating from yourself? Please, please, please try this before you read on. If you can achieve disassociation from disassociation, it will blow your mind.

One way to do this is to imagine you're sitting in a cinema watching a film of yourself on the screen. This is only the first level of disassociation, and so to go to the next stage, imagine that you're up in the projector booth, looking down on yourself watching yourself. Go on, do it now; can you see yourself looking at yourself?

OK, you disassociated from yourself disassociating i.e. you 'saw' yourself looking at yourself. Can you now go one final stage? Yes really. A stage that I've only managed to achieve a couple of times myself. Can you now disassociate from yourself disassociating from seeing yourself disassociate?

Hopefully you managed to perform these tricks of mental mastery, but you may now be left wondering what's the point of all of this, and how can you use it to help you?

Disassociation, remember, is a technique of removing yourself from the emotion and immediacy of a situation in order to take a more balanced, thoughtful and rational view of what is happening, and of how best to respond. When you disassociate at the first level i.e. seeing yourself in the situation, you are able to give yourself some advice as how best to respond, because you're looking at yourself from a second, slightly removed, position. When you disassociate at the second level i.e. the view from the projector booth, you are able to think about how you think about yourself. Thinking about your thinking.

An example might help make this clearer.

You were at a party last night, you got a bit drunk and ended up embarrassing yourself by saying a couple of things that you shouldn't have.

The next morning you go to stage one disassociation i.e. you play the mental video of last night's party and 'watch' yourself embarrassing yourself. You see yourself 'performing' and you also witness the reactions of people around you. From this removed position, both in space and time (it's the next morning, remember), you're able to give yourself some advice, and probably a bloody good telling off! You will almost certainly be feeling bad about your behaviour, which will further motivate you to heed your advice in future.

At 'Stage Two' disassociation, the next level, you think about how you are now thinking about yourself.

In the above example you might feel bad about the fact that you're feeling bad about your behaviour. You might resent the time you're spending mulling over your behaviour and mentally beating yourself up. This second level of removal could enable you to make a commitment to never feel bad about feeling bad again. Your mental dialogue may be something like... "I don't ever want to find myself in a situation again where I'm spending time feeling bad about something that I did, and which I could have prevented in the first place."

So Stage Two disassociation gives you a perspective on how you feel about your feelings.

The best advice I can give you now is to try this for yourself by thinking about a personal situation. It's no good relying on other people's examples, such as the one above; you have to practise on yourself.

Have fun, but don't stay 'out there' for too long. It can get lonely, and people will wonder where you are.

## Handling Direct Insults and Verbal Abuse

If you need help and advice on how to deal with physical attacks or how to disarm opponents using hand-to-hand contact, then once again this is not the book for you. If you find yourself in these situations regularly then you firstly need to ask yourself why either known or random people feel such compulsions to attack you. You then need to seek more radical solutions elsewhere. Chemical castration is an increasingly popular self-elected option.

Direct physical attacks aside, how about dealing with verbal attacks and insults?

There is no doubt about the power that words have to influence us, and when used with a deliberately malicious and negative intent they have the potential to 'cut deep'. The pain associated with being insulted can feel as searing as though a rapier has been thrust into your body. Even the language we use to describe such jibes 'cutting insults', 'cut to the quick', 'sliced my legs off' etc. reinforces the incisive and deadly power of such verbal attacks. If you doubt that you can be influenced linguistically then just ask yourself how you would react if someone came up to you in the street and said... "Hey *you*... Dick head!", or "Hey, come over here you arsehole!"

No-one's immune from such flagrant and brutish verbal attacks, and thankfully such direct abuse is rare, even in today's society. However, we have all been on the receiving end of situations where we have felt insulted, or we've heard of others who have suffered verbal abuse. The question is... how do we effectively deal with situations like this?

One of the first things to realise is that words themselves are not 'dirty'. After all, they're only words, a certain sequence of alphabet letters which go to create sounds.

The second thing to realise is that their power resides purely in how they're interpreted; and therein lies their 'Achilles' Heel', and the key to their effective diffusion.

If someone throws a ripe tomato at you or worse still, punches you in the face, then there's little doubt amongst bemused or amused onlookers about the impact that either the squishy fruit or fist made on your body. Alternatively, and this is the main point... if someone hurls an insult or aims a derogatory remark to you, then the impact this has upon you is entirely within your own control. Remember, you always have a choice in how you *use* words, and in how you *choose to react* to words that others use.

Sadly, when we find ourselves in situations such as this, there is little that we can do that would have any degree of likelihood of a successful and mutually rewarding outcome! The Rubicon has been crossed, there's no turning back, and little chance of rescuing the situation.

So, maybe for once (and we are near the end of the book), this is a case where the most appropriate response is simply to verbally fight back. However, remember the quote from Chapter Four...

> *"When you fight with a pig you both get dirty...*
> *...but the pig enjoys it!"*
>
> Unknown

If you do choose to fight back then it has to be because you've chosen to do so; it's a conscious decision. You have not allowed yourself to be dragged into an emotional fight; you've decided that enough's enough, and you're going to give as good as you get.

I used to work for the famous human relations training company, Dale Carnegie, which ran a series of workshops based upon the author's work. In one of his books 'How to Win Friends and Influence People', Dale talks about 23 principles for effective harmonious relationships. What he does not mention within the book, but which is covertly talked about by those within the organisation, is a 24th Principle, known as the 'wood chopping shed' principle.

The 24th principle states that... 'If you can honestly look yourself in the mirror, and say that you have really tried every single thing you can think about to work effectively with another person, and they are just not prepared to play along, then you can take them to the wood chopping shed and beat the s*** out of them!'

There you go; you have permission. Just don't send me the hospital bill.

I've tried everything else in this book so far, to prevent you from getting yourself into such destructive altercations.

So, review the previous pages and commit to taking action(s) well before you get to this stage.

Let's now lift things out of the gutter, and end with a more humorous look at the subject of insults. I hope that you, like me, will find some inspiration in the phrases below, and even get the opportunity to use some of them in the future.

## Just for Laughs

To end this chapter I've included a collection of responses that don't really belong anywhere else; either because they are humorous, just plain silly, or are likely to result in you receiving a violent slap!

So, put on your full body armour, and try out some of these:

### 1. Arrogant, Superior, Supercilious & Ostentatious

"I'm sorry, this might sound frightfully rude... but... should I know you?"

"And you are...?"

"I suggest you get 'your people' to talk with 'my people'."

"I'm sorry, I guess I hadn't bargained on a lack of basic competence."

### 2. Polite but clearly dismissive

"Well, I mustn't keep you."

"Before you go..."

"Thank you for your input."

"Would it be possible to speak to someone in authority here?"

[Yawning] "I'm sorry, it's not that you're boring me."

NB This is an example of a hidden suggestion

"Good God! Is that the time?"

## 3. Thinly Disguised Derision, Contempt and Ridicule

"That's certainly one way of looking at it Emily. [Turning to the wider group] What ideas do other people have?"

"That's certainly a unique perspective - I'll be sure to bear it in mind."

"I can see you feel strongly about this, but my mother always used to tell me that getting emotional was a sign of weakness."

"Well, I don't wish to be rude, but I do have an important light switch to mend."

"I'm not prepared to argue with you; but if it ever came to a choice of weapons, I would choose grammar."

"I'm sorry; I must have drifted off for a moment just then. What was it you were saying?"

"Who are you exactly...? God?"

"You have delusions of adequacy."

"Is that your coat?"

"You know where the door is... you came through it."

'With the greatest respect...' [not]

## 4. Blunt Rejection

"I'm sorry, were you talking to me or chewing a brick?"

"I'm sorry; I think you've confused me with someone who gives a shit!"

"Which part of 'No' do you not understand?"

## 5. Aggressive, Belligerent, Antagonistic and Hostile

"Are you always so objectionable, or are you singling me out for special attention?"

"I can see you have 'special needs'."

"I can now see why people say what they do about you."

"I don't need to take advice from anyone with the dress sense of a coat hanger."

"You're not only sitting in a sewer; you're adding to it."

"Steve, I'm really sorry, and this is awkward, but I think you need to know... I was just coming through Reception and I overheard some guy, I don't know who he was, talking about you and saying you were a 'wanker'."

"Why don't you just shut the f*** up!"

## And finally, some of the more famous insults of all time:

Bessie Braddock MP:  "*Winston – you are drunk.*"

Churchill:  "*Bessie, you're ugly, and tomorrow morning I shall be sober.*

Lady Astor:  "*Winston, if you were my husband, I should flavour your coffee with poison.*"

Churchill:  "*Madam, if I were your husband, I should gladly drink it.*"

"Your book is both good and original; but the parts that are good are not original, and the parts that are original are not good."

Samuel Johnson

"A freakish homunculus, germinated out of unlawful procreation."

Henry Arthur Jones; on Bernard Shaw

"If only he'd wash his neck, I'd wring it."

John Sparrow

"He can compress the most words into the smallest of ideas better than any man I ever met."

Abraham Lincoln

"He is a self-made man, and worships his creator."

Benjamin Disraeli (on John Bright)

"He is a modest little man, with much to be modest about."

Winston Churchill (on Clement Attlee)

"What time he can spare from the adornment of his person he devotes to the neglect of his duties."

Benjamin Jowett (on an undergraduate)

"From the moment I picked up your new novel, to when I laid it down I was convulsed with laughter. One day I intend reading it."

Groucho Marx

"Why don't you just sod off, you snivelling heap of Wombat's doo's."

Monty Python

# Chapter 10

## Mental Mastery & Strategies for Ecstasy

# 10
# Mental Mastery & Strategies for Ecstasy

Okay, this is the final chapter, and so I feel it's only right to end with a series of tools, strategies and tactics aimed to help us all to feel good.

I am also going to ask you to indulge me a little more, as I reveal some of my more esoteric thinking strategies; tricks of the mind if you like, that I've saved till the end. Tricks in the sense that they allow you to play psychological games with yourself, but not tricks in the sense of being 'tricky' or fake. I promise you that they all work for me, and I hope for you too.

So, let's start with… "Are you sitting comfortably?"

I ask because it's important that you're in the right state. A state of relaxation, comfort and curiosity would be a good combination, though others may be equally good. Can you do relaxation, comfort and curiosity? Can you get into that state right now?

Good, then let's begin.

## Getting Into a 'Right' State

What did you do just then? Did you do anything to attempt to change your state? Maybe you were already relaxed, comfortable and curious, in which case there was no need to change a thing. If you were not, then I am now the curious one, as I'm intrigued as to whether you changed anything to 'get yourself into' a different state?

If you were tense, uncomfortable and closed-minded then I would hope that you might at least have gone and grabbed a drink and a comfy cushion to deal with the first two. I'm taking it for granted that you're not closed-minded however, as you wouldn't have got to this stage in the book if you were; unless of course you're reading every word as you're planning on suing me.

So, true to form, let's follow this provocation with another:

---

**Provocation**   You can change your state at will.

---

There are some who claim that 'state is everything'.

What they mean by this is that your psychological state of mind is the single, most influential determinant of your outcomes. You don't have to think about this for too long to realise that whilst state may not literally be 'everything', it's certainly hugely important. How we feel and how we think at any given moment are massive determinants of how we behave, what we say, how we react to others and of what happens to us, and are therefore key to our outcomes.

Just compare how the result may be different if you go into a situation angry and fuming, looking for a fight or an argument, versus approaching the same scenario from a perspective of being calm, in control, curious and interested in how things will pan out?

So, if being in the 'right' state is so important, wouldn't it be great if, instead of being at the mercy of our natural psychological state of mind and its associated emotions, we were able to control and change our state at will? Well, as I pointed out above, we can. The first thing we need to do is to decide what state we want to be in?

## Decide Your State

When asked in a restaurant "How do you like your steak sir?" I always reply "Well done." Similarly, when it comes to "How do you like your state sir?" I cannot leave it to chance; I need to choose the right state, or combination of states for each situation.

Part of my life involves me working with groups in training workshops, facilitated discussion and experimenting with tools and ideas similar to the ones we've been exploring in this book. What states do you think the participants in such workshops should be in to gain the maximum benefit from the experience? After all, they've decided to be there, or even if they've been sent, they're devoting a day or so of their lives, so they might as well gain as much as they can whilst in the room.

I imagine that you came up with positive states similar to those listed below as being helpful to not only the individual themselves, but also to the facilitator and the other group members:

- Curiosity

- Receptiveness

- Intrigue

- Attentiveness

- Readiness to participate

- Open-minded

If, on the other hand you were about to sit an examination then you may want to retain some of the above, and would probably have a list that also included:

- Focused

- Clear headed

- Diligent

- Resourceful

- Calm

Finally, if you were about to stand up to do a presentation to a large group you may wish to be:

- Energised

- Confident

- Relaxed, but not complacent

- Enthusiastic

- Focused upon meeting the needs of your audience

- Optimistic of a positive outcome

| **Provocation**  | Choose your state(s). |
|---|---|
| | Don't simply default to, or fall into whatever state you happen to be wearing that day. Taking conscious control of your state of mind is one of the most fundamental techniques in the world of influence and persuasion. |

Developing the ability to direct and manage your state is the key to your main source of power... your ability to think, emote, speak, behave, respond and act, in the ways that you desire. You're effectively running your own brain; you're 'thinking about your thinking'.

From what you've learned so far in these pages you should, by now, have a pretty good idea about how to change and control your thinking, and therefore your state. However, there's one more thing that you can do to shift your state immediately, which is to change your physiology; your posture, your facial expressions and your movement.


## Fake It 'Till You Make It

We've already explored how to use the physiological actions of laughter and smiling to change state, based on the use of humour. To take things further we can now try to change our physiology to match the state that we want to experience. In general terms you're not going to want to generate negative, disempowering or stressful states. You're going to want to be, for example, more:

- Energised
- Confident
- Optimistic
- Determined
- Resilient
- Enthusiastic
- Communicative

Decide to banish, once and for all, disabling, paralysing, impotent and un-resourceful states from your behavioural repertoire.

Without deviating into acting lessons, the best advice I can give is to imagine the state that you want to have at a psychological level. Next, imagine how you would stand, sit, walk or hold yourself if you were in this state? How would you speak, breathe and project your voice? What would your tonality, your intonation, speech volume, pitch and pace be like? What expressions would you have on your face?

Once you've got a clear picture in your mind of what this looks and sounds like, then there's only one last step to achieving this state for real, and that's to act it out.

Yes, stand as you would stand if you felt confident, hold and move your hands and arms as you would if you were in full control. Breathe deeply and slowly, engage people with your eyes, speak in a controlled yet compelling and enthusiastic manner.

I call this the 'Fake it 'till you make it' technique.

 **Tactic:**   Change your physiology, and instantly change your state.

Strange as it may seem, acting out a state can actually produce that state... for real.

Once again, if you don't think this will work then it won't; because you won't even try it. So, as with all of these tactics, techniques and exercises, experiment with them and prove to yourself that they not only work, but that they're also immensely powerful.

## How Bad Do You Want To Feel?

Feeling bad takes so much effort; it can be physically and mentally draining. Why would anyone want to spend so much time and energy devoted to feeling bad?

If however, I really was determined to feel as bad as possible, would you be able to teach me how to do this? Could you tell me or show me what to do in order to feel lousy, rotten, fed-up, miserable, despondent, depressed or suicidal? After getting this far in the book you should be able to give me very clear instruction on:

- What I would have to think about, for how long and in what way?

- What I would have to do?

- How I should hold my body?

- What types of things I should talk to other people about?

- What facial expressions I should display to the world?

One day I came home to find my one of my sons sitting in the lounge alone, in a tense position, and with the biggest scowl on his face that anyone could humanly muster. I looked at him for a while, and even though I had come into the room he managed to hold onto this negative expression.

I was about to say to him something along the lines of… "What on Earth's the matter with you?", when I quickly changed tack and instead approached him with a look of intense curiosity and wonder on my own face. Crouching down beside him I looked directly at him and said… "Wow! How on Earth do you do that? It's amazing, that you're able to hold that expression for so long. You must have been practising for ages. Is it difficult?"

When someone's got themselves into such a bad mood they can become 'locked' into a state to the degree that it's very difficult, if not impossible, to get themselves out. You may have experienced this yourself, or know people who just can't help themselves.

My son was in just such a state that day because his mum had banned him from playing computer games; he was spending too long on them at the expense of doing his homework, something that I suspect many readers will identify with. I'm talking about the kids here, not adults... right?

So, I know that it was going to take a pretty special, potent and unusual technique to break the negative state that he'd got himself into. That's why I decided in that instant, to do what I did, because I knew that a more traditional approach would not only fail, it would probably make things worse. If I'd asked him what was wrong then all I would succeed in doing would be to direct his thoughts and negativity down the path of what was wrong, what was unfair, who was to blame etc. In the process I would be helping him to dig an even deeper pit of self-pity.

Another tactic that I've used in similar situations is to simply ask people:

*"How bad do you want to feel?"*

The question is so unusual that sometimes it alone is sufficient to do the trick. More often than not you will get a puzzled look and a question about what you mean? In which case, you follow it up by a secondary question of:

*"On a scale of 1 to 10, where 1 is 'just feeling a bit low', through 5 'pissed off', all the way up to '10' which represents 'hatred, inner deep-seated loathing, self-pity and resentment'... how bad would you like to feel?"*

These two questions may be enough to break their negative thought pattern, but you can go on with...

*"Have you not suffered enough already? Or do you think you deserve to be punished more by making yourself feel even worse by..."* [whatever they are doing e.g. dredging up bad memories up from the past, racking themselves with guilt, wallowing in negative thoughts etc.]

## 'Just Stop It' Technique

Recall the man from Chapter Five who went to the doctor?

Patient:    "Doctor, doctor."

Doctor:    "Yes, how can I help?"

Patient:    "It hurts whenever I reach my left arm over my left shoulder, bend it around the back of my head and grab hold of my nose from the other side."

Doctor:    "Have you thought about not doing that?"

Patient:    "Err, no."

Doctor:    "Well stop doing it then."

Patient:    "Okay, I'll try that. Thanks doctor."

The 'Just Stop It' technique is the most disarmingly simple method that I know of; so simple, in fact, that people either don't even think of it as an option, or they're so wrapped up in their condition that it needs someone else to point out the bleeding obvious.

If what you're doing isn't getting you what you want, or it's harming or hindering you in some way, then just stop doing it and try something else.

Be careful, techniques such as these are like a knife. They can be used to cut through negative states like a surgeon's scalpel, and to quickly leave the 'patient' much improved. However, knives can also be used to stab people.

Be cautious how you use your tools... and consider wearing 'eye protection'!

*"Careful son... you'll have someone's eye out with that!"*

Allegedly the last words of King Harold, King of Briton

---

**Tactics:**

Use the "How do you do that?" technique, or a variation on the theme, to snap people out of negative states.

Use the 'On a scale of 1 to 10' technique.

Use the 'Just stop it' technique.

Because you're using unusual and provocative techniques, be prepared for unpredictable reactions and responses – take precautions.

---

So, from all of the above, we understand that state is critical, and anything that threatens our positive states is to be resisted, just as one would resist an enemy.


## Enemy of the State

I'm not referring to Will Smith, but rather the nay-sayers, whiners, whingers, complainers and no-hopers of this world who, no matter what you do or say, are immensely capable of sapping every last drop of enthusiasm, optimism and good humour out of you.

You know who they are; the 'Dementors' as I call them, borrowing the descriptor from J.K Rowling's Harry Potter tales. As soon as they walk into a room the temperature drops 5 degrees, they then proceed to drain all the happiness from their victim, and in extreme cases even steal their soul.

I am not going to waste my time or yours in coming up with '10 Top Tips' for dealing with people like this. I have just one simple piece of advice for you with respect to these people and, assuming you're not married to one of them, it's:

---

**Provocation**     Avoid 'Dementors'.

---

Sadly, if you are in a long-term relationship with someone like this, or who has become like this, then you have a more difficult decision to make.

Some people don't want you to solve their problems, because as soon as you do they won't have anything left to moan about, and moaning is their favourite hobby. What an interesting psychological oxymoron... 'Not being happy unless you're moaning'.

So, just (politely) stay out of their way, and instead, focus your time and energy on a much more profitable activity which we will now explore... the personal manufacture of controlled psychoactive substances.

## Start Your Own Personal 'LSD Factory'

You no longer need to worry about the street price of cannabis, or whether your supply of cocaine will last until the end of the weekend. And you can ditch the Rohypnol; what are you doing with that stuff anyway?

The best drugs are 'free' because you can make them yourself without any special equipment, and only the knowledge contained within this book. The only drawback is you can't package them or sell them on.

Amongst the pharmaceuticals that you can legally manufacture are substances such as LSD, morphine, adrenaline and other naturally occurring endorphins. You can also run off a steady stream of dopamine or serotonin, designer drugs if you like, just to suit you. But the advantages don't end there. Personally manufactured drugs are guaranteed to be 100% pure, so there's no risk that they've been 'cut' with soap powder, or some more dangerous substance, and no-one can arrest you for manufacturing or taking them. In fact you don't even need to go to the bother of carrying needles, swabs, razor blades mirrors or other paraphernalia around with you, as they are self-administering.

If you've not already guessed, I'm talking about the human body's natural ability to manufacture a whole range of psycho-active chemicals, including the feel-good ones listed above. Sports enthusiasts will easily identify with the phenomenon of the 'runners' high', the positive, mood-enhancing effect of engaging in physical exercise. It's referred to as the runner's high but it applies to any physical sport that's played at a relatively high level of exertion. So, how we generate and control our state brings us back to physiology again, and reveals our next practical tactic:

**Tactic:**  Engage in strenuous, regular physical exercise. Not only will you improve your health and fitness, you will also release a stream of post-exercise 'feel-good' chemicals into your bloodstream.

## Laughter – the Best Medicine

When was the last time you laughed so hard and for so long that you cried, or your internal muscles ached with exertion? I will never forget, and neither will my friends, the time I laughed so loud and for so long that I was forced to lie on my back on the floor kicking my legs in the air. It was the only way I could stop the pain from killing my stomach muscles. After about 20 minutes it became tiresome for my friends, but I remained convulsed in a state of helpless, paralytic excruciating ecstasy for twice as long.

Here are a couple of exercises that don't involve you doing the 'dying fly', but which can help you to feel good – instantly.

There are only two situations when you can do these exercises safely. The first is if you are with a group of like-minded individuals who are keen to try it out. The second is when you know for sure that you are alone and no one is likely to hear you or walk in on you.

 **Exercise 1:**

This one's easy. All you have to do is to laugh out loud, as though you've just been told a hilarious joke or watched the funniest comedy sketch on television. Now you aren't laughing naturally and spontaneously; you're faking it. Go on, try it now. Really pump it out, and keep it going for at least 15 – 20 seconds.

The moment you stop, try to think about something that in the past made you depressed.

If you applied yourself to the exercise diligently they you should find that your feelings about the depressing thought have lightened a little, become less intense or powerful, and they may even have changed. You're feeling better, and for no reason.

Admittedly you're not going to change reality with psychokinetic tricks such as these. However, in Chapter Eight we discussed the fact that your reality is made up of your combined perceptions about something whether it's real or not, and so in a sense, you *are* changing reality, by altering your internal reality.

We know that when we feel better we tend to smile, and we don't need a research paper to prove it to us. However, we spoke earlier about the link between physiology and thinking, and research has also shown that it works the other way around. Smiling actually makes us feel better because smiling can trigger the release of serotonin in the brain, a naturally occurring neuro-transmitter that makes us feel good. Again, you don't require a research paper to prove it because you can try it out right here, right now.

 ### Exercise 2:

This one's even easier, but it is very, very silly, so be warned.

If you're alone then lift your head up high and put on the most amazingly expressive and broad smile you can imagine. Hold it for several seconds, and then experiment by alternating between a whole range of outrageously happy, smiley and beaming expressions. You really, do need to make sure that you are not being watched when you do this, as you will have great difficulty convincing an ill-informed onlooker that you're not bonkers.

If you are with a co-operative friend, or better still in a group, you should sit side by side and on the count of three, simultaneously turn to each other (in pairs if you are in a group), with a huge smile. It helps enormously if, as you turn towards each other, you both make the sound of an elongated 'e', as in...

## "eeeeeeeeeeeee"

Now remember, I said that this is silly, but if you think it's stupid, then I will forcibly disagree with you.

There's a huge difference between something that's 'silly' and something that's 'stupid'. Silly things are just harmless fun, which may or may not be helpful. For example, silly games at parties or the humour typified by comedians such as the Goons or Monty Python is definitely in the silly bracket, and certainly helps in the laughter and good feelings stakes. Silly things may be banal or childish, but they are generally not destructive.

Stupid things however, are just plain stupid i.e. not only do they serve no purpose, they're also ill-advised and often damaging. Stupid things don't achieve the outcome you want, and can even take you in exactly the wrong direction. Intelligent people do not repeat stupid actions; that would be doubly stupid.

---

**Tactics:**  Try the laughing exercise; if nothing else, just doing it might make you laugh for real because it's so silly, and then you won't be faking the laughter any more.

Try the smiling exercise; either alone with a mirror in the privacy of your own home, or with a small group of consenting adults.

Better still, try it with children; they'll love it and in return they'll *naturally* make you laugh.

---

Laughing at your laughing, thinking about your thinking, feeling angry about getting angry... all of these are proven and legitimate psychological techniques which can be grouped under the collective term 'apply to self'.

## Bring Me Sunshine

Many readers will also recognise the part that sunlight plays in helping us to feel good. In particular, sunlight has been proven to have a positive effect upon people with a particular type of depression known as Seasonal Affected Disorder (SAD). In this 'unhealthy market' there's a healthy market in 'light boxes' designed to give sufferers artificial exposure to sunlight, particularly during the winter months when the real thing is hard to come by.

So, this is another simple, practical action that you can take to help you to feel better, whether you are noticeably SAD or not.

> **Tactic:** Get a healthy dose of sunshine when you can.
>
>  Yes, I know that you shouldn't get sunburnt, and so should you, so I'm not going to patronize you with an overly zealous and unnecessary health warning.

Feeling good is good, but feeling great is terrific.

What else can we do to both improve our state of mind, and to help others improve theirs, and therefore release even more mind-lifting drug boosts to our system?

Well, we can practise getting ourselves into a wonderful state, and then getting other's around us into a similarly wonderful state. You don't even need to know these people, as it works just as effectively with strangers in hotels, shops, restaurants, or just about anywhere you come into contact with other people.

Go up and talk to people; ask them a question; make a humorous observation; take an active interest in what's going on around you, commit to saying "Yes" more often to things that might be fun; and be proactive in initiating a conversation. Many people in social situations are shy to do so, and most are happy and relieved when someone else (you) takes the initiative to engage.

## How Much Pleasure Can You Stand?

There's more to happiness than just laughing and smiling, whether this be in the company of others, or alone in your attic!

As we've already begun to explore, there's a range of inspirational or ecstatic states that you can get yourself into, including curiosity, delight, excitement, wonder, awe etc.

If you fill your life with activities that generate these states, and spend time with other people engaging in tasks and situations that create uplifting feelings, then you'll find that you and those around you will have very little time to feel depressed. It could be as simple as watching your favourite comedy show, reading a funny book, spending an enjoyable evening in the pub with friends, playing a musical instrument or simply going for a brisk walk on a sunny autumn day with your dog. You don't even need a dog – just borrow someone else's, they will be eternally grateful. Neither do you need me to give you a list of enjoyable mood-enhancing activities, you know yourself what makes you feel good, so:

> **Tactic:**  Make a list of at least 30 things that you could do that you know make you feel good.
>
> Stick it somewhere prominent, such as on the fridge or the back of the toilet door, and commit to doing at least one of those things on the list each and every day.

Even saints knew how to enjoy themselves in their time:

> *"Sorrow can be alleviated by a warm bath and a good sleep....*
> *...preceded by a glass of wine."*
>
> Thomas Aquinas

So we can, and should pack our days with feel-good activities, but the reality of life and work means that we cannot block our eyes to the hum drum normality of living, or just getting through the day, and in particular dealing with things that go wrong. So what else can we do to help us deal with current or recent difficult or distressing events?

Let's take a trip back from the future.

## Back From the Future

How far into the future do you need to mentally transport yourself before you can 'look back' on a painful memory or current situation and it won't bother you any more?

Okay, it depends on the event, and in some cases we may still feel pain five, ten or even more years later on, particularly with events such as the death of a close family member.

However, if we confine ourselves to less dramatic situations, when you look back on this in six, nine, twelve or a hundred months from now, how significant or important do you think it will be when viewed from that fresh, future perspective? My guess is not very much, if at all; certainly it will have been drained of vivid details and emotional energy, and so much more will have happened in your life.

The singer songwriter Anastasia put it well when she sang... *"I'm sick and tired of feeling sick and tired."* [another example of 'apply to self'.]

Would you prefer to think about current or recent troublesome situations from that future-oriented, diluted and impotent way right now? Assuming you would find this helpful, here's how to do it.

*NB: The passage you are about to read may not make perfect grammatical sense; this is deliberate, as I have designed it to help you to see things in a new light.*

*Imagine going forward in time, say five years, and metaphorically 'look back' on the situation as it is today. You've moved on in many ways in the last five years, and so many things are now different. You're also wiser, more mature, you have a more complete and broader perspective on life, and you've been practising the 'Water off a Duck's Back' techniques diligently and successfully since then. As you look back, now, and attempt to recall what it used to be like when you were faced with the situation, and you see it, now, as a rather fuzzy, distant, small black and white image, how insignificant does it now seem in the grand scheme of things? How much less important and obscure is it, and how vague and unconnected do you now feel in relation to those distant emotions, which, as you think about them now, are increasingly difficult to remember, aren't they? They were, weren't they, and even now, as*

*you think about it you wonder why it was that you bothered to let it occupy your mind in the past, quite so much... didn't it?*

Once you've satisfied yourself that from this new perspective the incident is merely a shadow of its former self, simply 'pull' that future perspective into today, and decide to think about it in this new way from this point forwards. You've already thought about it in this way, haven't you, so you can do it can't you, so all you need to do now is to remember to think about it in this new, more helpful way again, won't you.

All you're doing is using your current perspective of your future perspective a little ahead of its time. That's fine; you're already adept at pulling perspectives from the past into the present and feeling just as bad today as you did then, so isn't it fair to do it both ways and to re-balance things a little?

Does this make sense? If not, why not read the above three paragraphs again until they start to make more sense – *didn't they!*

'Back From The Future' is a sophisticated, yet powerfully simple technique which is now part of your broader toolkit for getting things into their proper context and perspective, a topic we first discussed in Chapter Five.

---

**Tactic:** Use the 'Back From The Future' technique to reduce the painfulness of recent events.

---

So that's using the future to help us to gain a more useful perspective on the present. What else can we do, that's a little more physical or provocative, to deal with how we're thinking about things right now?

## 'Shove It Up Your Arse!'

Forgive the title of this section, but I promise you the original title was much worse, and I'm sure my publisher would have rejected the whole book because of just five words. The whole point of this technique is that it *has* to be provocative, because it relies upon shock and provocation in order to work. Think about it as X-Rated HSBC adverts if you like.

We discussed in Chapter Six how we constantly use unspoken internal dialogue to talk privately to ourselves. That's fine if it's positively powerful and uplifting, but some people fill their heads with negative self-talk, either criticising themselves for some personal failure or inadequacy, or imagining ahead of time, things going horribly wrong – this is *very* common.

For example, have you ever been for a job interview and worried about being late, about getting tongue-tied, not being able to answer a question or embarrassing yourself? What about going to a party where you don't know many people. Do you visualise yourself standing awkwardly in a corner, nursing a warm glass of white wine with nobody talking to you, whilst speed-eating nuts? What about an important presentation you need to do at work? Do you imagine yourself going to pieces in front of the audience? You will, if the little devil in your head has painted a negative picture of what's going to go wrong.

Why do most people choose to fill their heads with unhelpful, negative self-talk, which only serves to heighten any apprehension about the situation, and thereby put themselves into an unhelpful state – even before they've experienced the event itself? It's not big, it's not clever, it's not helping you and you have to stop it right now.

Unfortunately just catching yourself and trying to stop it is not good enough, as we've discovered that these corrosive thoughts have a tendency to creep back in. We discussed several strategies and tactics in Chapter Six to deal with this, but now we're ready for the Big Daddy of strategies.

If you want someone to go away you sometimes have to tell them in the strongest terms possible, or they won't get the message. So, my tactic to shut up purveyors of negative internal dialogue is to verbally tell them to 'go away' (I use stronger language than this). Yes, I mean that I physically shout it out loud, even though the voices are in my head and completely self-manufactured.

Now, here's the biggest Health Warning of all:

##   Health Warning

Ensure that you are not in a place where you can be overheard.

When I first discovered this strategy I called it my 'Formula F1' technique, for reasons that I will keep to myself. Such was its power when I first tried it out, it has stayed with me for more than ten years, and never fails me.

If it helps, imagine that there's a naughty little leprechaun inside your head (the source of these infernal internal negative voices), and you've now had enough of listening to their negative, harmful, depressing and whinging dialogue. It's time to scream at him to shove it where the sun doesn't shine!

If he's not helping you with uplifting, positive thoughts and advice, but rather bringing you down by making you feel inadequate or bad in some way, then that voice in your head is doing you massive internal damage, and you need to change it or chuck it out for good.

> **Tactic:** Use the 'Shove It Up Your Arse' vocal technique to banish the leprechauns from your mind.
>
> Ensure that you:
>
> - Physically shout it out (where you can)
>
> - Do it every time you catch the negative voices speaking to you
>
> - Have fun in the process!

Remember though, you can't 'think of nothing', so once you've ex-communicated the little blighter you need to replace his destructive dialogue with something more positive and encouraging.

Bring on the 'Gospel Choir'...

## Employ a Gospel Choir and 32-Piece Orchestra

In the negatively framed interview, party and presentation examples referred to earlier, we might replace:

*"What if she doesn't like me."*

with...

"She's dying to meet me and I know she's going to like me."

Replace...

*"What if I can't answer their questions?"*

with...

"Boy, they're going to be so impressed with my background, experience and achievements they can't fail to want to give me this job."

Replace...

> *"How can I get out of going to the party?"*

> with...

"'This is a great opportunity to get to meet some new people, to have a laugh and to chill out. I'm going to be so busy chatting with people, I won't have time to eat nuts."

Now, just like Wagner, you don't want to be playing this audio track on a tinny little tape recorder. You need the backing of a full-blown 32-piece orchestra, and to hear your new positive internal dialogue punched out by a 100 strong gospel choir!

Try it now, kick out the leprechaun with the strongest language you can muster, then pump up the volume and feel the floor beneath your feet vibrating as you hear your new self-talk being punched out by 100 overexcited evangelists! It's all in your mind, and you're not paying for a single note so have 500 evangelists if you like and a 300 piece orchestra. Nothing's going to drown that lot out!

## *"Hallelujah!"*

---

**Tactic:**   Use the 'Gospel Choir' technique to install new, empowering
    thoughts and positive self-talk.

---

## Take a Free Holiday

Earlier we discussed how you can pull positive perspectives from the future in order to diminish the strength of current ill feeling. Building on this technique, you will now realise that you can easily create memories of things that haven't yet happened? You can even remember things that will never happen. How can this be so, and more importantly how can it help you?

In fact, you're already accomplished at doing this; it's just that many people do it the wrong way around. We've just talked about the interviewee who, days before the meeting runs through mental images of it not going well, of being asked questions that they can't answer, and ultimately failing to secure the job. What impact do you think this mentally made up memory of an imaginary future has on the thinker? Not only will it mean that they go into the interview in a negative frame of mind, it also means that they're going to be feeling bad now, and in the days leading up to the event. How stupid is that?

But how does any of this help us to get a free holiday?

Think about what happens when you think about a holiday that you've planned and booked, and that might not be occurring for several months? I'm simply asking you to think about your thinking.

If you're like most people, you will think about your future holiday on multiple occasions in the months leading up to the event. As the date approaches the frequency and intensity of your imaginings will increase, and you will find yourself getting quite excited. Your thinking is now beginning to affect your mood and your emotions. When you get closer to packing time you will be thinking about it in some detail, imagining the scene, what the weather will be like, what you will wear, what you will do, the local attractions you will visit, the beaches or people you will lie on or the slopes that you will ski down. The day before your holiday your mind will be filled with positive images and excited anticipation, you're likely to be energised and motivated, and generally in a good mood.

And the holiday hasn't even started!

When my kids were younger they used to get so excited as Christmas approached. In fact, my daughter began running her mental movies as early as November. As soon as the first Christmas trees started to be cut she was desperate for us to get one, even though it was only 5th December and the tree would be dead by Christmas Eve if we got one then.

The point I'm making with these two stories is that often the anticipation of a positive event is as good, if not cumulatively better, than the event itself. If you could add up all the positive thinking episodes leading up to your holiday, and compress them together, the total amount of sheer mental pleasure might easily be greater than that which you get from the event itself.

In writing this section I decided to experiment further with the idea, so that I could communicate to you in as vivid and pragmatic a way as possible, both how this works, and the extent to which you can take control of your thinking and emotions.

The example I've just personally experimented with is an imaginary ski trip. In other words I imagined a skiing trip that I haven't even booked, and certainly which won't cost me any money. I am going to use this real example to illustrate three levels of thinking:

Level 1:  Thinking about something exciting - in this case going skiing.

Level 2:  Getting excited about your thoughts of skiing, as you imagine
yourself skiing down mountains. If you really have booked a ski trip,
you simply get excited about thinking about the fact that you are
going skiing in a few weeks time. If you haven't booked a trip then
you can still get excited about thinking about skiing down mountains
– just use your imagination.

Level 3:  Getting excited about the fact that you are getting excited about
thinking about skiing... *bear with me on this one.*

So, I've just experimented with this myself, and in the space of just a couple
of minutes I worked myself up into a heightened state of excitement, not only
about skiing, but also about the power of this mental gymnastic technique.

This is what has just happened in my brain in the last 2 or 3 minutes...

I thought about skiing holidays that I had been on in previous years (it helps,
but is not essential, if you have had a similar experience in the past).

I began to get excited about the prospect of a holiday as I filled my mind with
vivid images, sounds and positive feelings from previous skiing trips.

As my excitement rose (within about 10 seconds) I decided to see if I could
get excited about the fact that I was getting excited. 20 seconds into the
experiment and my level of excitement had risen to a new level. I felt my
mind racing, my heart rate rising, my level of mental alertness heightening
and my whole demeanour changing.

I turned to speak to my son who was working in the same room to tell him
about my excitement in thinking about the holiday, and about how excited I
was feeling about my level of excitement. As I spoke to him my voice level

and speed of speech rose, I felt myself getting carried away with the level of energy and enthusiasm that I was putting into what I was telling him.

I then started to laugh at how silly this whole thing seemed, but I was also laughing because I could hardly believe how easy and effective this technique was – it was actually working! As I laughed, I found this only served to push my level of excitement further and I then (now this is approaching something akin to an out of body experience) started to laugh at the fact that it was making me laugh – remember we discussed this earlier.

Before long my son was laughing too, two positive emotions for the price of one.

> **Tactic:** Use the 'Remember an Imaginary Positive Future' technique.

## It gets better...

Just as you can derive as much value and enjoyment from the anticipation of a holiday or future pleasurable event, as you can from the event itself, it's possible to extract even more value from two additional perspectives, that's four different sources of excitement:

1. **In the future**, the excitement that you will experience from the event itself – let's call this 'real time' excitement, and the one we can most readily identify with.

2. **In the near future** as your excitement grows – the excitement associated with your anticipation of future excitement, as discussed above.

3. **Right now**, as you feel excited about how excited you feel about all of this; your level of excitement excites you, which in itself is quite exciting.

4. **After the event**, as you recall and re-live in your mind, and vividly recount to others, the positive aspects of the event. This is the "I can dine out on this for weeks" scenario. This is creating excitement from remembered excitement; again, very real, very beneficial mood-enhancing excitement that you're generating for free, from just one past event.

If you have a real event that's far into the future then pull it forward in time in your mind and imagine it happening right now. This cannot fail to raise your level of excitement.

Having just related this technique to my other son, he decided to go one stage further and asked whether it would be possible to get excited about getting excited about my level of excitement?

I thought about this for a couple of seconds and then tried it out. With a little bit of mental squirming, and some more challenging gymnastics (thinking about my thinking about my thinking about something) I am delighted to report that I managed to achieve this too, if only fleetingly.

It's normal to be initially confused by these progressive levels of abstraction as we're stretching our cognitive abilities way beyond the levels of thinking in which we normally engage. In Chapter Nine we engaged in a similar disassociation exercise when we learned how to handle direct criticism. However, as I've discovered to my delight, it's possible to become good at using techniques such as these remarkably quickly, provided you try them out and are prepared to try again if your first attempt doesn't quite work.

Experiment with these neurological tricks yourself, and let me know how you get on at jon@blueiceconsulting.co.uk

**Note:**

Remember, you're not making up memories simply to pretend that they're true; you're not deluding yourself – that would be stupid. You're making up 'memories' that serve you. Whether they're true or not is irrelevant; if they make you feel good then that's reason enough; the end justifies the means.

Think of it as deliberate, orchestrated dreaming. A wonderful dream can still leave you feeling wonderful about magical imagined memories... that you know never happened.

Here's another personal story, from twelve years ago, which taught me a powerful technique, which again, I have used on numerous occasions to help me to stay relatively mentally healthy.

## Change 'Irritators' Into 'Inspirators'

When our kids were very young, my wife and I bought a new, farmhouse pine kitchen table. I was paranoid that the monsters (sorry, little darlings) would damage it by sticking cutlery into the soft pine surface, draw on it with indelible marker pens, drop heavy toys on it or in some other ways damage our lovely new table.

The inevitable happened. What else was I to expect in a busy household with a baby a toddler and a young child? Over the course of the next few weeks the table became progressively marked, dented, spilled upon, stained and even the odd chunk was taken out of it. Every night I would come home from work, walk into the kitchen, see another bit of damage and then automatically go into rant mode... "Who's done that?" I would demand. "Why can't anyone look after things around here? I'm sick and tired of coming home and finding yet more damage to the table; I wish we hadn't bought it in the first place."

You can imagine the predictable scene unfolding every tea-time. I was making myself feel bad, and not only me. What a great mood for a young family to see Dad return home in. It didn't exactly promote healthy and happy relationships.

Everything changed when I decided to change my response to the stimulus of yet more damage to the table (remember Viktor Frankl). Quite simply I decided consciously and deliberately to feel 'good' every time I discovered another piece of damage. I decided to choose and change my chain reaction.

But surely I'm just fooling myself; after all, the table's still getting damaged; it sounds crazy. Maybe it *sounds* crazy, but in terms of benefits to me and my family it was one of the most practical, pragmatic, sensible and positively beneficial decisions I could have taken.

This is a personal example of the 'silly but not stupid' law in action; on the surface a silly thing to think or do, but underneath, sensible and beneficial to everyone. Why? Because it worked.

What I found even more surprising was the speed with which this happened. When I made a decision to view my table not as something new that had become damaged, but as something old and characterful, a natural product of a busy working family kitchen, the effect was transformational and instantaneous. I also reasoned that people often pay good money just to have that well-used, distressed look imparted upon pieces of furniture. Our table is now worth twice what we paid for it.

> **Tactic:** Reverse how you *think* about something and you will
>  immediately reverse how you *feel* about it, and a whole lot
> else will change besides.

Now enough about you and me; how about everyone else? To close this chapter, and the book, what can we do to make the world a better place?

## Make Someone Else Feel Good

Before anyone accuses me of contradicting an earlier assertion, 'Nobody can make you feel anything without your permission', then please note that the key words are 'without your permission'.

When you're in the business of helping people to feel good, then you're not likely to come up against active resistance, unless of course you're dealing with a 'Dementor', and I've already told you not to waste your time on them (but see below, for what you *can* do with them).

It's quite amazing how you can positively influence another person's mood; optimistic attitudes, positive energy and enthusiasm tend to be infectious. Borrowing the title of the last section you could decide to be an 'Inspirator' yourself, rather than an 'Irritator', an energy-giver, not an energy-sapper, a mentor rather than a Dementor.

## 'Expecto Patronum'

Right at the start of this book I told you that you were going to get your 'magician's wand' out. Well now it's time to close the 'magic circle' with a spell from the world of Harry Potter.

*"So,"* said Professor Lupin. *"The spell I am going to try and teach you is highly advanced magic, Harry – well beyond Ordinary Wizarding Level. It is called the Patronus Charm."*

*"How does it work?"* said Harry nervously.

*"Well, when it works correctly, it conjures up a Patronus,"* said Lupin, *"which is a kind of Anti-Dementor – a guardian which acts as a shield between you and the Dementor."*

*"The Patronus is a kind of positive force, a projection of the very things that the Dementor feeds upon – hope, happiness, the desire to survive – but it cannot feel despair, as real humans can, so the Dementors can't hurt it."*

*"But I must warn you, Harry, that the Charm might be too advanced for you. Many qualified wizards have difficulty with it."*

J.K.Rowling – 'Harry Potter and the Prisoner of Azkabarn (1999)

If you're feeling particularly Wizardly today, and up for challenge, then I suppose you could always go and find the crankiest person you can, and try to make them feel wonderful; be a Patronus for a day. You could always justify the investment of your time with a Dementor on the grounds of clinical research and personal education. In addition to providing you with a stretching sociological experiment, you will no doubt derive some pleasure from the challenge.

Remember however, you can't encourage anyone else to be happy unless you're prepared to be happy yourself. You have to 'go there first' if you want to affect people's feelings. That's why I started this chapter by talking about your own state, and how you can control it. You won't stand a chance of eliciting positive emotions from people if you're feeling depressed yourself, if you think that life sucks or you walk through life sucking energy from it yourself.

So, get yourself sorted out first, and then make it your life's mission to help other people to feel good about themselves; become one of life's Patronus'.

J.K. Rowling's Dementors aside, who are truly evil, most people are not inherently bad; they often just don't know any better. Like you, they're struggling in their own way to make the best of their lot. Unfortunately they often go about it in the wrong way. When cornered they lash out, when they're in a negotiation they think 'Win-Lose' rather than 'Win-Win', when trying to influence they don't have half the tools in their kitbag that they need, and even then, they don't know how to use them wisely.

Finally, this is not a purely altruistic appeal to you. If you're going to do things to help people to feel good, then you'll feel good yourself; you won't be able to help it. Half the fun of Christmas is seeing other people open the presents that you have bought for them. The more good you share, and the better you feel, the more your life is going to shine; you won't be able to stop it. Good things will happen to you and you will attract people *because* you make them feel good.

Which brings us neatly to our final Tactic...

# Final Tactic:

*Make someone feel good...*

*Just because you can*

Notes

Notes

Notes

Notes

Notes

Notes

Notes